DIPS dollops
and drizzles

DIPS dollops
and drizzles

Liz Franklin

PAVILION

For my Mum and Dad.

For teaching me to delight in good food,
and because I love you both so very much.

xx

First published in Great Britain in 2000 by
PAVILION BOOKS LIMITED
London House, Great Eastern Wharf
Parkgate Road, London SW11 4NQ

Text © Liz Franklin 2000
Design and layout © Pavilion Books Ltd

Photography by Ian Wallace 2000

The moral right of the author and illustrator has been asserted

Designed by Isobel Gillan

A CIP catalogue record for this book is available
from the British Library.

ISBN 1 86205 456 8

Set in Rotis
Printed in Singapore by Tien Wah Press

2 4 6 8 10 9 7 5 3 1

This book can be ordered direct from the publisher. Please contact
the Marketing Department. But try your bookshop first.

contents

introduction

D*ips, Dollops and Drizzles* is all about beautiful but doable food. It's all about relaxing, fun mealtimes, when dunking into something delicious and dipping into carefree chatter with friends and family make the perfect combination – the kind of times you'll look back on fondly for years to come.

Complicated recipes with long instructions and endless lists of ingredients often disappoint, yet just a modest drizzle of truffle oil can lift a plain dish of pasta to new heights. A plump sun-ripened fig becomes a sumptuous dessert served with nothing more than an ice-cold dollop of thick Greek yoghurt and a lick of sweet honey. And a pretty bowl of fruity olive oil in which to plunge crisp, young vegetables and salad leaves can bring a circle of friends together for an evening to remember.

Tempting, easily-achievable food is the essence of this book, and for inspiration I have reached out to many corners of the world. Helped by the diverse range of ingredients now widely available in supermarkets and specialist shops, I have encompassed the exotic flavours of Japan, Indonesia, Thailand, China and India. In addition to combining trusted favourites such as lemon grass, ginger and star anise, I have included relative newcomers to Western cuisine such as tamarind and shiso. Some of the recipes capture the essence of Mediterranean cuisine, with sun-drenched vegetables and pungent herbs. From North Africa, I have taken the tender, piquant flesh of salt-preserved lemons, and from Iran and the Middle East, tart sour-sweet pomegranate molasses.

A delicious dip represents food at its most convivial and undemanding. Watch how the first eager dip of a small child's finger into a bowl of chocolaty cake mixture reveals the sheer pleasure of touching, scooping and sharing good things to eat. It is a pleasure that seldom leaves us, even as we grow older. The dips that I have featured in this book offer a versatile and truly sociable way in which to enjoy great food and good times with friends for every occasion, from intimate suppers to parties for a crowd. Among my favourite times are casual evenings sat around the kitchen table with good company, chilled wine, and warm grissini to plunge into glistening bowls of Tapenade, or crisp Sardinian Parchment Bread to snap and dunk into dishes of richly flavoured Tomato, Mascarpone and Fresh Basil Dip. I love to see the delighted faces when I begin a dinner party with salt-crusted shot glasses filled with Tequila Lime Dip and served with long, elegant skewers of Salt-Chilli Prawns or end it with a pretty cup of Cappuccino Dip. The dips can be made in advance, and for many of them this brings extra benefits as subtle, sleepy seasonings develop lively and pronounced flavours.

The most basic of foods can become truly exquisite when dressed quite simply with natural, enticing flavours. Just as a fluffy jacket potato can seem incomplete without creamy golden butter, a generous dollop of tangy chutney or a fruity salsa can give new character to a piece of fish or meat and bring the flavours of a far-off country magically into your home.

And in much the same way that a trickle of cream over warm apple pie can add a touch of luxury, a drizzle of something quite simple can transform an everyday dish into a special and well-loved treat. The drizzle recipes I share here are much less complicated than classic sauces, but they are rich with exciting and tempting flavours, from vibrant Spicy Tomato Drizzle to luxurious Buttery Caper Drizzle.

To complement each recipe, I have included an array of unusual and delicious accompaniments, from crisp biscuits, tarts and breads to sticky skewers of meat and freshly cooked fish. I love the chewy Mango-Leather Scoops, created with an old-fashioned method of preserving, whereby fruit purée is dried out slowly in the oven overnight: so simple because the oven does the work while you sleep, but so stunning and distinctive to serve with sweet dips. For lazy days or busy days don't be afraid to substitute shop-bought goodies.

Feel confident to mix and match throughout the book, as I do. Horseradish Potatoes are great with fillet steak, but fabulous with pan-fried salmon as well. Grand Marnier Cream is lovely with Little Ginger Puddings, yet dreamy over juicy summer strawberries.

Grant yourself poetic licence. If your fruit is a little less sweet, your appetite a tad larger, or numbers somewhat greater than I have allowed for don't be afraid to give a tweak here or a twiddle there. If your oven takes its time, or belts out heat like a blast furnace, just give the temperature a gentle nudge up or down. Let your instinct and your palate be your guides.

Most of all, have fun and enjoy! I wish you good times and great food.

Equipment

Many kitchen gadgets and gizmos have passed my way over the years – indeed one of the jobs I do is testing them! If I had to choose my favourites, especially in the context of this book, first would be a good sturdy food processor with the usual attachments for blending and mixing, whisking, chopping and kneading – a great time saver for the busy cook. Then a deep-fat fryer; although I don't use it every day, it sizzles and seals enough to earn its keep and is great for featherlight Cinnamon Puffs and Warm Lover's Knots. And I would have to be dragged kicking and screaming from my ice cream machine – I would so miss the gorgeous ices that it makes!

larder basics

A larder built upon good foundations will always show in your cooking. It's much better to use a small amount of a high-quality ingredient than to be generous with something second-rate. Here are some of the basics I like to keep at hand...

Anchovies
Buy anchovy fillets preserved in olive oil – they're great for flavouring sauces, mayonnaise and dips.

Butter
Good-quality butter will enhance your cooking – margarine will ruin it.

Capers
Capers add a lovely piquant note to dressings and sauces. Look out for them salted or pickled in sherry vinegar.

Cheese
Parmesan cheese is fabulous for fresh basil pesto and for grating and shaving into all manner of things. Buy it in blocks and grate as needed. Soft cheeses such as ricotta and mascarpone are versatile for both sweet and savoury dips and dollops.

Cocoa powder
Use pure, dark cocoa powder for baking and dusting.

Concentrated orange juice
I always like to keep a couple of small drums of concentrated, unsweetened orange juice in my freezer. This is the kind you need to top up with water. If used undiluted, they add a lovely, intense flavour to sauces and custards.

Eggs
Buy organic, free-range eggs rather than battery-produced if possible, as the flavour is superior and the risk of salmonella significantly reduced. Organic free-range eggs come from hens who are alllowed to roam free and fed a totally natural diet without drugs. This tends to lessen the risk of disease immeasurably.

Garlic

Crucial! For adding flavour to a wide variety of savoury dishes.

Herbs

Fresh herbs can make such a difference to a variety of sweet and savoury dishes. They have a much better flavour and texture than dried herbs (with the exception of bay leaves), and a garnish of fresh herbs can make even the simplest dish sensational. If you don't have herbs in your garden, why not grow little pots on the kitchen windowsill or outside your kitchen door? My favourites are basil, bay, chives, coriander, mint, parsley, rosemary and thyme.

Horseradish (creamed)

Terrific for making Horseradish Potatoes (see page 50).

Lemons (fresh and preserved)

Fresh lemons are a firm fixture in my kitchen. When a recipe calls for the zest, try to use organic, unwaxed lemons – they have a nicer flavour.

Tangy preserved lemons are invaluable, too, for adding a burst of concentrated lemon flavour to a recipe. They are easy to make at home. Quarter fresh lemons, leaving them intact at the base. Pack a tablespoonful of coarse sea salt inside each lemon and squash into tall airtight (Kilner) jars. Leave for 3–4 weeks before using, turning the jar occasionally. The salt

and juice develop into lemony brine and the peel becomes tender and luscious. Top up the jar with extra lemon juice and olive oil.

Mustard

Smooth Dijon and wholegrain mustards will add a tasty kick to umpteen dishes.

Oils

Extra virgin olive oil is invaluable in the kitchen. I like to keep small bottles flavoured with herbs, chillies and roasted red peppers. Occasionally I will use sunflower oil for frying or preparing mayonnaise.

Olives

Great for chopping into dressings and drizzles, for Tapenade (see page 28) and simply for nibbling!

Pine nuts

Essential for making classic Italian pesto. These can deteriorate if stored for too long so do keep them in the fridge.

Salt

I always use natural sea salt: flakes for sprinkling and coarse for grinding.

Sauces

Good-quality tomato ketchup, Worcester sauce, Japanese soy sauce and Indonesian sweet soy sauce are brilliant for making quick marinades, dips and drizzles.

Spices

Wherever possible, buy spices whole and grind them just before using. Among the most useful are whole black peppercorns, dried chillies, cinnamon sticks, coriander seeds, cumin seeds, fennel seeds, ground ginger, whole nutmeg and star anise.

Tomatoes

Tinned chopped tomatoes are brilliant for making sauces and dips. Good-quality sun-dried tomatoes in olive oil are great for enriching sauces, dips and roasted vegetables.

Better still are home-dried tomatoes! Slice firm but ripe tomatoes in half lengthways and lay them cut side up on a large roasting tray. Sprinkle with a pinch of sugar, some salt flakes and a grinding of black pepper. Scatter over a little fresh thyme, add a drizzle of olive oil and leave overnight in a very low oven (140°C/275°F/Gas 1). If you're not tempted to eat the lot for breakfast the following day – store them in clean airtight jars, covered in olive oil.

Vinegars

Red wine and white wine vinegars are super for dressings and splashing into sauces. Good-quality balsamic vinegar is worth its weight in gold, and if you can add some luscious fruit vinegars, such as raspberry, all the better.

Yoghurt

Greek yoghurt is fabulous for simple dips, stirred through with chopped herbs or fruit purée, and makes a lovely alternative to cream with desserts.

dips

Dips are about food at its most convivial
and undemanding. There is an innate pleasure to
be found in touching, scooping and sharing
nice things to eat. The delights in this chapter, both
savoury and sweet, will unfold a truly delectable
and versatile way in which to share great food and
good fun with friends, for every occasion.

pinzimonio

This dip is striking in its flavours and yet surprising in its simplicity. Good-quality extra virgin olive oil is very lightly seasoned and accompanied by an array of crunchy vegetables (*crudités*) set on ice. I first fell in love with this popular Italian appetiser in a hilltop family restaurant in Sardinia. The food was undemanding yet quite delectable, and the relaxed but lively atmosphere buzzed with the chatter of native Sardinians, many of whom enjoyed Pinzimonio between courses as a palate cleanser.

SERVES 4

for the dip

200 ml/7 fl oz/scant 1 cup good-quality
  fruity extra virgin olive oil
salt and freshly ground black pepper

for the *crudités*

a selection of fresh young vegetables of your
  choice, such as:
4 long, young, very fresh carrots, peeled

3 sticks celery, trimmed
1 red (bell) pepper, topped, tailed
  and deseeded
1 yellow (bell) pepper, topped, tailed
  and deseeded
1 orange (bell) pepper, topped, tailed
  and deseeded
2 bulbs Florence fennel
1 radicchio di Verona (round red-leafed
  chicory), washed
2 handfuls ice cubes

To make the dip, pour a little extra virgin olive oil into each of 4 small dishes, and season lightly with a little salt and freshly ground black pepper.

For the *crudités*, prepare the carrots, celery and peppers by cutting them into long, thin, elegant strips of about 13 cm/5 in. Remove the leafy fronds from the fennel, peel away any tough or stringy outside leaves, trim the base and cut in half. Cut lengthways into slices.

Take a large, decorative bowl and lay the ice on the bottom. Separate the leaves of the radicchio, wash and dry them and then line the sides of the bowl with them. Arrange the vegetable strips attractively on top of the ice in the dish. Serve immediately with the bowls of seasoned olive oil.

stilton and port jelly dip
with cracked pepper crunchies

This cheese dip is topped with a layer of sparkling port-wine jelly and makes a perfect dinner-party starter. I like to serve it in individual bowls, with Cracked-Pepper Crunchies and some plump black grapes.

SERVES 4

for the dip

115 g/4 oz/¹⁄₂ cup cream cheese
140 ml/4¹⁄₂ fl oz/scant ²⁄₃ cup soured cream
150 g/5 oz/1¹⁄₂ cups Stilton cheese
1 stick celery, very finely chopped
1 tbsp fresh chives, very finely chopped
¹⁄₂ leaf gelatine

5 tbsp port
¹⁄₂ tsp caster (superfine) sugar
2–3 drops fresh lemon juice

for the crunchies

3 slices thin-cut, day-old bread
3 tbsp olive oil
cracked black peppercorns

Preheat the oven to 190°C/375°F/Gas 5.

To make the dip, whiz together the cream cheese and soured cream in a food processor. Add the Stilton and whiz again. Transfer the mixture to a bowl and add the celery and chives. Mix thoroughly. Divide the mixture between 4 small ramekins and smooth the tops over carefully. Refrigerate to chill.

Meanwhile, place the gelatine in a little cold water and set aside to soften for 3–4 minutes. Pour the port into a small pan, add the sugar and lemon juice, and heat the mixture very gently until it is just warm and the caster sugar has dissolved. Remove the pan from the heat. Squeeze the excess water from the gelatine and add it to the warm port mixture in the pan. Stir, until the gelatine is thoroughly dissolved. Allow the mixture to cool; as it does, it will start to thicken. When the port mixture is cold, spoon it over the cheese. Refrigerate until the jelly has set.

For the crunchies, cut the crusts from the bread and toast lightly. Carefully cut the bread horizontally and place on a baking sheet. Brush with a little olive oil and sprinkle very lightly with cracked black peppercorns. Bake for 5–10 minutes until crunchy. The crunchies can be made several hours in advance and stored in an airtight tin. Serve with the Stilton and Port Jelly Dip.

roasted red pepper dip
with oven baked tortilla crisps

Creamy soft cheese and roasted peppers make a wonderful dip. For a
rich but mellow dip, roast the peppers in olive oil. For a dip with a
little more bite, use pepper oil or sprinkle a small deseeded and finely
chopped red chilli over the peppers before roasting.

SERVES 4

for the dip

4 large red peppers, topped, tailed and
  deseeded
3 cloves garlic, crushed
4 tbsp olive oil or pepper oil
salt and freshly ground black pepper
400 g/14 oz/1¾ cups cream cheese

for the crisps

8 small flour tortillas
2 tbsp olive oil

white or black sesame seeds, cracked pepper
  and sea salt for sprinkling

Preheat the oven to 190°C/375°F/Gas 5.

To make the dip, begin by roasting the red peppers. Cut them into thin strips
and lay them in a shallow ovenproof dish. Scatter the crushed garlic over them
and drizzle over the oil. Season with a little salt and a touch of black pepper.
Roast for 40 minutes or until the strips of pepper are soft and dotted with
charred bits on the edges. Remove from the oven and leave to cool.

Place all but 1 tablespoonful of the peppers, their cooking juices and the
cream cheese into a blender or food processor and process until you have a
smooth mixture. If the dip seems a little thick, add an extra trickle of olive oil.
Transfer the mixture to a pretty bowl or individual ramekins, garnish with the
remaining strips of roasted pepper and serve.

For the tortilla crisps, brush the tortillas with a little olive oil and sprinkle with
white or black sesame seeds, or cracked pepper and a little sea salt. Cut each
tortilla into 4 pieces and lay on baking trays. Place in the oven for 5–10 minutes
and cook until golden brown. The tortillas will crisp up as they cool. They can be
made several hours in advance if necessary and stored in an airtight tin. Serve
with the Roasted Red Pepper Dip.

tomato, mascarpone and fresh basil dip
with sardinian parchment bread

The rich flavours of Italy bubble down here to make this my favourite dip. Serve with wafer-thin pieces of Sardinian Parchment Bread.

SERVES 4

for the dip

3 tbsp olive oil

1 large onion, finely chopped

2 cloves garlic, crushed

1 × 400 g/14 oz/large tin chopped tomatoes

1 tsp caster (superfine) sugar

salt and freshly ground black pepper

2 tbsp mascarpone cheese

generous handful fresh basil, torn

for the bread

300 g/11 oz/2¾ cups plain (all-purpose) flour, sieved

200 g/7 oz fine polenta

2 tsp salt

freshly cracked black peppercorns (optional)

2 tbsp rosemary, freshly chopped

300 ml/10 fl oz/1½ cups warm water

Preheat the oven to 220°C/425°F/Gas 7.

To make the dip, heat the oil in a pan over a gentle heat and sauté the onions and garlic until soft but not brown. Add the tomatoes and the sugar. Stir and season. Bubble for 10 minutes until it becomes thick and has a rich red colour.

Add the mascarpone and stir. Add lots of basil. Transfer to a food processor and whiz briefly so that the dip retains a chunky texture. Serve warm.

For the bread, place the flour in a large bowl and add the polenta. Add the salt and pepper (if using) and stir in the rosemary. Add enough water to make a firm (but not sticky) dough and knead into a smooth ball. Turn the dough out on to a lightly floured surface and break off a piece of dough about the size of a golf ball. Roll it out until very, very thin – almost transparent. Repeat until all the dough is used up.

Bake for 2–3 minutes, until golden brown. Carefully turn the bread over and cook for a further minute or so. Remove from the oven and leave to cool.

To serve, spoon the dip into a special bowl, and surround with large, crisp sheets of Sardinian Parchment Bread.

tonnato dip
with rosemary-chicken swizzle sticks

Based on the Italian speciality Tonnato sauce (usually served with veal), this creamy dip is perfect with grilled skewers of chicken marinated with garlic and rosemary.

SERVES 4

(MAKES 20 CHICKEN STICKS)

2 tbsp fresh parsley, chopped

salt and freshly ground black pepper

for the dip

1 egg

1 tsp Dijon mustard

zest 1 lemon

1 tbsp fresh lemon juice

300 ml/10 fl oz/1½ cups sunflower oil

1 × 90 g/3½ oz/small tin tuna in oil, drained

2 tbsp capers, finely chopped

½ red (bell) pepper, finely diced

for the chicken sticks

3 fresh skinless, boneless chicken breasts

juice ½ lemon

2 cloves garlic, crushed

1 tbsp chopped fresh rosemary

3–4 tbsp olive oil

20 bamboo skewers
  (soaked in cold water for half an hour)

To make the dip, place the egg, mustard, lemon zest, juice and salt in a food processor, then whiz to blend. Slowly add the oil until the mixture is thick and light and looks like mayonnaise. Add the tuna and capers and process again until you have a smooth mixture. Transfer to a bowl and stir in the chopped pepper and parsley. Check the seasoning and adjust if necessary. Turn out into a pretty bowl and refrigerate until required.

Soak the bamboo sticks in water for thirty minutes before using, to prevent them scorching under the grill.

For the chicken sticks, cut the chicken breasts into 1 cm/½ in strips and thread on to the soaked bamboo skewers, twisting the chicken slightly as you go. Place them in a shallow dish and squeeze over the lemon juice. Scatter with the crushed garlic, the rosemary and drizzle over the olive oil. Season with salt and freshly ground black pepper. Cover and marinate for an hour or so. Grill until golden brown and cooked through.

Serve with the Tonnato dip.

spicy butternut dip
with onion-seed bagel crisps

This is a great dip for squash lovers – lightly spiced and slightly sweet all at the same time. Scatter black onion seeds over shop-bought bagels and oven bake to transform them into crunchy crisps.

SERVES 4

for the dip

1 fairly large butternut squash
1 tbsp olive oil
1 tbsp cumin seeds
1 tbsp coriander seeds
1 tsp fennel seeds
1 tsp black onion seeds (Nigella seeds)
1 tsp black mustard seeds
2 cloves garlic, crushed

1 × 5 cm/2 in piece fresh ginger, finely
  chopped
2 tbsp Greek yoghurt
2 tbsp mango chutney
dash Tabasco
salt and freshly ground black pepper

for the crisps

3 fresh bagels
2 tbsp olive oil
2 tsp black onion seeds (Nigella seeds)

Preheat the oven to 200°C/400°F/Gas 6.

To make the dip, cut the squash in half along its length and remove the seeds. Score a criss-cross pattern across the cut surface of each half with the point of a sharp knife. Place on a baking tray and drizzle over olive oil. Roast in the oven for about 40 minutes, until soft and golden.

Meanwhile, toast the spices lightly in a small pan until they give off a spicy, nutty aroma (take care not to burn them or they make the dip taste bitter). Remove the squash from the oven and place in a food processor with the garlic, ginger, yoghurt, chutney and toasted spices. Whiz until you have a thick purée. Add a dash of Tabasco and season to taste with salt and black pepper.

Turn out into a bowl and set aside until required. This dip is best served warm or at room temperature.

For the crisps, cut each bagel into wafer-thin slices. Place the slices on baking sheets and brush with olive oil. Scatter each piece with a few onion seeds. Turn the oven temperature to 190°C/375°F/Gas 5 and bake for 10 minutes or until golden. Allow to cool and become crisp.

Serve with the Spicy Butternut Dip.

tequila lime dip
with salt-chilli prawns

The inspiration for this dip came from the famous Tequila Slammer, with its combination of salt, lime juice and Tequila. The prawns are cooked quickly until crisp but succulent, then speared on to long, elegant bamboo skewers. For a special touch, serve the dip in shot glasses that have been frosted with flakes of coarse sea salt.

SERVES 4

(MAKES 24 SKEWERS)

for the frosting

1 egg white

coarse salt flakes

for the dip

100 ml/3½ fl oz/scant ½ cup Tequila

zest 1 fresh lime

juice ½ lime

2 tbsp caster (superfine) sugar

for the prawns

90 g/3½ oz/1½ cups fresh breadcrumbs

2 tsp chilli flakes

2 cloves garlic

salt and freshly ground black pepper

24 raw tiger prawns, peeled and deveined

2 egg whites, lightly whisked

oil for frying

24 bamboo skewers

To decorate the glasses, pour the egg white on to a large plate and whip lightly with a fork. Pour some flaked sea salt in an even layer on to another plate. Dip the rim of each glass into the egg white and then briefly into the salt. Leave to dry.

To make the dip, combine the Tequila, lime zest and juice and the caster sugar and stir well. Refrigerate until required.

For the prawns, mix the breadcrumbs, chilli flakes and garlic together in a bowl, then season with salt and freshly ground black pepper. Dip each prawn into a little egg white and then into the breadcrumb mixture to coat. Heat a little oil in a wok or heavy-based frying pan and deep-fry the prawns for 2–3 minutes on each side until crisp, golden and cooked through. Drain on kitchen paper.

Spear each prawn with a bamboo stick and serve with the Tequila Lime Dip.

tamarind and apricot dip
with sticky pork fingers

Tamarind is a fruit used widely in Indian and Chinese cuisine; it has a tart sweet-sour flavour that makes a delicious addition to many dishes. In this dark, glossy dip I have used ready-prepared tamarind paste, which is now easily found in most major supermarkets.

SERVES 4
(MAKES ABOUT 20 FINGERS)

for the dip

300 ml/10 fl oz/1½ cups well-flavoured
   chicken stock
2 tsp tamarind paste
1 tbsp Indonesian sweet soy sauce
   (ketjap manis)
4 tbsp good-quality apricot conserve
1 tbsp wholegrain mustard

for the fingers

400 g/14 oz minced pork
2 cloves garlic, crushed
1 medium onion, finely chopped
4 tbsp Worcester sauce
2 tbsp dark soy sauce
1 tsp wholegrain mustard
salt and freshly ground black pepper
2 tbsp fresh coriander (cilantro),
   finely chopped

bamboo skewers

To make the dip, place the chicken stock, tamarind paste, sweet soy sauce, apricot conserve and mustard in a pan and bubble over a low heat until reduced by about half, when the mixture should be glossy and have thickened to the consistency of pouring cream. Set aside.

Place the pork, garlic, onion, Worcester sauce and dark soy sauce in a food processor and whiz until well mixed together. Add the mustard, season with salt and freshly ground pepper and stir in the fresh coriander. Mix everything thoroughly, then form into little finger shapes, roughly the size of mini sausages (which incidentally are perfect with this dip if you are short of time!).

Fry the pork fingers in a little hot oil until golden brown and cooked through.

Thread on to bamboo skewers and serve immediately with the Tamarind and Apricot Dip.

yoghurt and coriander dip
with spicy lamb nuggets

Creamy Greek yoghurt makes a lovely dip when partnered with a little pungent garlic and aromatic fresh coriander. It makes an ideal quick dip when combined with spicy shop-bought crisps, and with little nuggets of lamb, this velvety dip is simply divine.

SERVES 4

(MAKES ABOUT 20 NUGGETS)

for the dip

400 ml/14 fl oz/1²/₃ cups Greek yoghurt

2 fat cloves garlic, crushed

2 tbsp fresh coriander (cilantro),
  finely chopped

for the nuggets

375 g/13 oz minced lamb

1 clove garlic, crushed

1 medium onion, finely chopped

1 tsp ground ginger

2 tsp cumin seeds

1 tsp coriander seeds

2 tbsp Worcester sauce

2 tbsp soy sauce

1 tbsp fresh coriander (cilantro),
  finely chopped

oil for frying

bamboo skewers

To make the dip, mix the yoghurt, garlic and coriander in a bowl and set aside for 30 minutes or so, to allow the flavours to develop.

For the nuggets, place the lamb, garlic, onion and ginger in a food processor and whiz until everything is combined.

Toast the cumin and coriander seeds in a small pan until they begin to release a lovely aroma. Crush the seeds lightly using a pestle and mortar and add them to the lamb mixture. Stir in the Worcester sauce, soy sauce and fresh coriander.

Form the mixture into small balls and fry in a little hot oil until golden brown and cooked through. Drain on kitchen paper and thread on to bamboo skewers.

Serve immediately with Yoghurt and Coriander Dip.

japanese plum dip
with skewered sesame salmon

A large supermarket or a good deli will provide all the ingredients for this delicious oriental-style recipe. Japanese plum vinegar is a zesty, slightly sour creation made from Japanese ume plums with the brilliant red leaves of the shiso herb. Furikake seasoning (pronounced furry car key!) is a combination of white and dark sesame seeds, Nori seaweed and dried shiso leaves. Palm sugar has a rich toffee flavour and is produced from the sap of the coconut palm, but if you can't find it, soft brown sugar can be used instead.

SERVES 4

(MAKES ABOUT 20 SQUARES)

for the dip

6 tbsp Japanese plum vinegar

1 tbsp Worcester sauce

1 tbsp palm sugar

1 tbsp fresh coriander (cilantro),
  finely chopped

small piece spring onion, very finely sliced

for the salmon

zest ½ lemon

35 g/1¼ oz Japanese Furikake seasoning

4 × 150 g/5 oz salmon fillets, skinned
  and boned

sea salt

1 egg white, lightly whisked

bamboo skewers

To make the dip, mix the plum vinegar, Worcester sauce and palm sugar together and stir well. Add the coriander and a couple of small spring onion rings, then pour into small oriental dipping-sauce bowls.

Mix the lemon zest with the Furikake seasoning and spread over a large plate. Cut the salmon into bite-size pieces. Lightly season the salmon, brush the top and bottom of each square with a little egg white and coat with Furikake seasoning, leaving the sides free to expose the blush-pink colour of the salmon.

Pan-fry the salmon in a little hot oil for about 2 minutes on each side, or until cooked but still slightly opaque in the centre. Remove from the pan and drain on a little kitchen paper.

Thread on to bamboo skewers and serve immediately with the Japanese Plum Dip.

black olive tapenade
with rosemary and olive oil grissini

SERVES 4–6

for the dip

2 fat cloves garlic, crushed

2 tbsp capers

6 tinned anchovy fillets, drained

1 tsp fresh thyme, chopped

small handful fresh basil leaves

250 g/9 oz/2 cups pitted
  black olives

zest and juice 1 unwaxed lemon

5 tbsp olive oil

salt and freshly ground
  black pepper

for the grissini

15 g/½ oz fresh yeast

1 tsp caster (superfine) sugar

300 ml/10 fl oz/1½ cups
  warm water

450 g/1 lb/4 cups strong plain
  (all-purpose) flour, sieved

1 tsp salt

2 tbsp fresh rosemary,
  finely chopped

1 tbsp olive oil

I love Tapenade, with its salty, tangy flavours and versatility. Bowls of glistening black or green olive Tapenade always remind me of my favourite olive stall at the early morning market in Aix-en-Provence, where huge bowls of sumptuous Tapenade sit waiting to be eaten.

Preheat the oven to 200°C/400°F/Gas 6.

To make the tapenade, place the garlic, capers, anchovies, herbs, olives and lemon zest and juice in a food processor and whiz until you have a paste. Add the olive oil and whiz again. The paste should be smooth. Season with a little salt and black pepper to taste. Set aside to allow the flavours to develop.

For the grissini, put the yeast and sugar into a small bowl and crush together until you have a smooth paste. Add 100ml/3½ fl oz/scant ½ cup of the warm water, cover and leave for 15 minutes, after which the yeast should be frothy.

Place the flour and salt in a large bowl and stir in the chopped rosemary. Make a well in the centre and pour in the yeast mixture, olive oil and remaining water. Stir well, incorporating all the flour to form a soft (but not sticky) dough. Knead for 10 minutes until the dough is smooth and elastic. Lightly oil a large plastic bag and place the dough in it. Leave in a warm place for 1–2 hours, until doubled in size.

Knead again for 5 minutes. Take small balls of dough and shape into long thin sausage shapes. Place on a baking sheet and bake for 8–10 minutes until golden brown and crisp. Transfer to a wire rack to cool.

Serve with Black Olive Tapenade.

sweet lime dip
with chocolate tuiles

This delightful dip consists of light, fluffy cheese flavoured with zesty lime and a trace of mint. Try combining it with crisp, chocolaty tuiles for a fabulous but easy dessert.

SERVES 4

(MAKES 12 TUILES)

for the dip

100 ml/3½ fl oz/scant ½ cup water
75 g/3 oz/scant ½ cup caster (superfine)
  sugar
juice 3 fresh limes
400 g/14 oz/1¾ cups cream cheese
1 tbsp mint, freshly chopped

for the tuiles

50 g/2 oz/¼ cup butter, softened
75 g/3 oz/scant ½ cup caster (superfine)
  sugar
50 g/2 oz/½ cup plain (all-purpose) flour,
  sieved
1 tbsp good-quality cocoa powder
1 egg white

icing sugar to dust

Preheat the oven to 190°C/375°/Gas 5.

To make the dip, place the water, sugar and lime juice in a pan and simmer gently for a couple of minutes or so until the sugar has melted and the syrup has thickened slightly. Remove from the heat and leave to cool. Place the cream cheese in a blender and add the lime syrup. Whiz everything together until you have a smooth mixture. Add the mint and whiz for a moment or two more. Turn out into 4 individual dishes or ramekins or a large bowl.

For the tuiles, mix the softened butter, sugar, flour, cocoa powder and egg white together until smooth. Spread the mixture very thinly in oval shapes on lightly oiled baking sheets. Bake for 3–4 minutes, until firm.

Remove from the oven. Quickly lift each tuile from the tray and place straight on a rolling pin, coaxing the sides gently around the pin to create a curved effect. They should be crisp after 2–3 minutes. The tuiles can be made several hours in advance and stored in an airtight tin.

Just before serving, dust with a little icing sugar and serve with tangy Sweet Lime Dip.

dreamy chocolate dip
with coconut ice cream nuggets

These little nuggets of coconut ice cream dunked into this oh-so-easy dip make a delightfully different dessert that reminds me of my favourite chocolate coconut bar.

SERVES 4

for the ice cream

300 ml/10 fl oz/1½ cups coconut milk
40 g/1½ oz/½ cup desiccated coconut
4 egg yolks
115 g/4 oz/½ cup caster (superfine) sugar
150 ml/5 fl oz/⅔ cup double (heavy) cream
2 tbsp Malibu liqueur

for the dip

300 g/11 oz good-quality milk chocolate
2 tbsp Malibu liqueur

cocktail sticks

You will need an ice cream machine

Make the ice cream in advance, to allow time for freezing. To make the ice cream, put the coconut milk and the desiccated coconut in a pan and heat until it is almost boiling.

In a large bowl, mix the egg yolks and caster sugar together. Slowly pour the hot milk into the egg mixture and stir well. Pour everything back into the pan. Stir constantly over a low heat until the mixture is thick enough to leave a trail when a finger is drawn along the back of the spoon. Be careful not to let the mixture boil or the eggs will scramble and the texture of the ice cream will be very grainy.

Remove the mixture from the heat, and add the double cream and Malibu liqueur. Leave to cool, then transfer to an ice cream machine and churn until frozen. Using a melon baller, scoop out little balls of ice cream and place in the freezer until ready to serve.

For the dip, break the chocolate into squares and place in a bowl with the Malibu liqueur. Stir gently over a pan of barely simmering water until the chocolate has melted. Divide between 4 individual dessert dishes or ramekins.

Remove the coconut ice cream nuggets from the freezer, spear each with a cocktail stick and serve immediately with the Dreamy Chocolate Dip.

greek yoghurt and raspberry-ripple dip
with crispy cinnamon puffs

This eye-catching dip of creamy yoghurt marbled with tangy raspberry purée can be served with crisp, warm cinnamon puffs for an exquisite combination of flavours.

To make the dip, place the Greek yoghurt in a bowl and stir in the caster sugar. Whiz the raspberries in a food processor, until you have a purée and sieve to remove the seeds. Stir in the caster sugar and taste to check sweetness. Swirl the purée through the yoghurt. Turn into 4 small bowls or 1 serving bowl.

For the cinnamon sugar, mix the sugar and cinnamon together.

For the cinnamon puffs, place the butter and water in a pan and bring to the boil. Remove from the heat. Mix together the flour, salt, sugar and orange zest. Slowly pour this into the butter and water mixture, stirring constantly. Return the pan to the heat and beat with a wooden spoon until the mixture is smooth and forms a ball in the centre, leaving the sides of the pan clean. Remove from the heat. Allow the mixture to cool a little and then slowly add the beaten eggs, stirring well until they are all incorporated and the mixture is shiny. Leave the mixture until cold and then form into walnut-sized balls.

Deep fry at 190°C/375°F/Gas 5 for 4–5 minutes until golden brown and puffy. Drain on a kitchen towel and toss in the cinnamon sugar.

Serve while warm with the Greek Yoghurt and Raspberry-Ripple Dip.

SERVES 4

for the dip

550 ml/18 fl oz/2½ cups thick
  Greek yoghurt
1 tbsp caster (superfine) sugar

for the purée

200 g/7 oz/1 cup
  fresh raspberries
40 g/1½ oz/3 tbsp caster
  (superfine) sugar (or to taste)

for the cinnamon sugar

50 g/2 oz/¼ cup caster
  (superfine) sugar
1 tsp ground cinnamon

for the puffs

50 g/2 oz/¼ cup butter
125 ml/4 fl oz/½ cup water
75 g/3 oz/⅔ cup plain (all-
  purpose) flour, sieved
pinch salt
½ tsp caster (superfine) sugar
zest 1 unwaxed orange
2 eggs, beaten

peach and ricotta dip
with warm lover's knots

This sublime dip combined with warm Lover's Knots is perfect for dinner parties and special occasions.

Lover's Knots are fried strips of sweetened dough that are eaten in Italy to celebrate *Carnivale*, a festival just before Lent. Throughout the regions, they have different names including such delights as *nastri delle suore* (nun's ribbons) and *cenci* (rags and tatters).

SERVES 4

for the dip

2 ripe but firm peaches
50 g/2 oz/¼ cup caster (superfine) sugar
250 g/9 oz/scant 1¼ cups ricotta cheese
2 tbsp peach liqueur

for the lover's knots

250 g/9 oz/2½ cups plain (all-purpose) flour, sieved
pinch salt
40 g/1½ oz/3 tbsp caster (superfine) sugar
finely chopped zest and juice 1 orange
2 tbsp orange liqueur
1 egg
1 egg yolk
40 g/1½ oz/3 tbsp butter, melted

oil for deep-frying
caster (superfine) sugar to dust

To make the dip, place the peaches, sugar, ricotta and peach liqueur in a food processor and whiz until you have a smooth mixture. Turn out into an attractive bowl and refrigerate until required.

For the Lover's Knots, place all the ingredients in the bowl of a food processor and blend until you have a smooth (but not soggy) dough. Form into a ball, cover with cling film and leave to rest for an hour or so if possible.

Roll the dough out on a floured work surface until it is about 5 mm/¼ in thick, then cut ribbons of dough 1 cm/½ in wide and about 8 cm/3½ in long. Carefully tie a knot in the centre of each ribbon. Heat some oil to 190°C/375°F/Gas 5 and fry in small batches until crisp and golden.

Drain on kitchen paper, dust lightly with caster sugar and serve immediately with the Peach and Ricotta Dip.

cappuccino dip
with chocolate coated spoons

This dip has a beautiful cappuccino flavour and looks stunning served in little coffee cups and dusted with chocolate to imitate the much-loved frothy Italian coffee. Crisp biscuits and tuiles make a lovely accompaniment, but for a special touch – try coffee spoons that have been dipped into dark Belgian chocolate.

SERVES 4

for the coffee layer

4 large egg yolks

65 g/2½ oz/⅓ cup caster (superfine) sugar

1 tbsp very strong coffee (I use espresso or 1 heaped tbsp good-quality coffee granules mixed with 1tbsp boiling water)

1 tbsp Kahlua or Tia Maria liqueur

425 ml/15fl oz/scant 2 cups double (heavy) cream

for the cappuccino layer

2 leaves gelatine

4 tbsp cold water

250 ml/8 fl oz/1 cup milk

50 ml/2 fl oz/¼ cup double (heavy) cream

1 tbsp caster (superfine) sugar

for the spoons

50 g/2 oz dark Belgian Chocolate (minimum 55% cocoa solids ideally)

4 pretty coffee spoons
4 small coffee cups or ramekins

continued overleaf   sweet dips   **37**

To allow for setting, you will need to make the dip 4 or 5 hours in advance. In a large bowl, mix the egg yolks and the caster sugar thoroughly. Add the coffee and Kahlua or Tia Maria liqueur and stir. Pour the cream into a medium-sized pan and heat until the cream starts to bubble at the edges – not quite at boiling point. Remove the pan from the heat and slowly pour the hot cream into the egg mixture, stirring gently.

Now place the pan back over a low heat and stir until the mixture thickens: this should take 2 or 3 minutes. Don't be tempted to turn the heat up – the mixture will curdle and spoil. To determine when the mixture has reached the right consistency, draw a finger along the back of the spoon. If it leaves a clear line the mixture is thick enough. Pour the mixture through a sieve into a clean bowl or jug and then fill the coffee cups or ramekins.

Leave the coffee mixture to set and make the topping. Break the gelatine leaves up and place in a small bowl. Cover with the cold water and leave to soak for 4 or 5 minutes. In the meantime, pour the milk and cream into a small pan and add the sugar. Heat the mixture gently until the sugar has melted but do not allow the mixture to boil. Remove from the heat. Squeeze the excess water out of the gelatine leaves and add them to the mixture in the pan. Stir thoroughly until the gelatine has melted and the mixture is smooth. Pour the mixture through a sieve into a clean bowl and refigerate to set.

When the milk mixture has set, whisk it for a minute or so to create a light, frothy effect that mimics the topping on a cappuccino. Carefully pour a little of this mixture on to each of the coffee dips and leave to set for 4 or 5 hours, or overnight.

For the spoons, break the chocolate up into a bowl and set this over a pan of barely simmering water. When the chocolate has melted, remove the bowl from the heat and dip each spoon into the chocolate to coat. Line a small, smooth baking tray with cling film and lay the spoons carefully on this to dry. When the spoons have set, peel away the cling film and store them in a cool, dry place until required. The Chocolate spoons can be made several hours ahead and stored in a cool, dry place.

vin santo
with cherry and pistachio *biscotti*

Vin Santo is a rich Italian liqueur wine, often used as the wine for Holy Communion. These cookies, flecked with sour cherries and pistachios soak up Vin Santo and make the tastebuds tingle.

MAKES ABOUT 40 COOKIES

for the dip

1 tbsp egg white
1 tbsp caster (superfine) sugar
Vin Santo

for the *biscotti*

300 g/11 oz/2½ cups plain (all-purpose)
  flour, sieved
1 tsp baking powder
50 g/2 oz/¼ cup butter
130 g/4½ oz/⅔ cup caster (superfine) sugar
150 g/5 oz/1¼ cups unsalted pistachio nuts
115 g/4 oz/½ cup dried sour cherries
3 eggs
1 tsp almond extract
1 tsp natural lime extract

To make the dip, lightly whisk the egg white and pour it on to a small side plate. Sprinkle the caster sugar on to another small side plate. Dip the rim of each glass briefly into the egg white and then into the caster sugar. Leave to dry.

Make the *biscotti* in advance and store them in an airtight tin. Mix the flour and baking powder together and rub in the butter until the mixture resembles fine breadcrumbs. Add the sugar, pistachio nuts and cherries, and stir. Whisk the eggs together with the almond and lime extracts and add this to the flour mixture. Form the mixture into a ball, making sure that the mixture is stiff but not dry. Divide the mixture in half and roll each half into sausage shapes about 4 cm/1½ in in diameter and place onto baking trays. Bake for about 20–25 minutes until golden brown and firm. Remove from the oven and leave to cool.

Cut the cooked *biscotti* dough into thin slices and place on baking sheets. Bake for 10–15 minutes at 170°C/325°F/Gas 3 until golden brown and crisp. Remove from the oven, leave to cool and store in an airtight container.

When you're ready to serve the pudding, carefully pour the Vin Santo into the frosted glasses, taking care not to wet the rims, and serve with the *biscotti*.

papaya and coconut dips
with cinnamon brandy snaps

This is an exquisite dip as the colourful orange hues of papaya offer a delightful contrast to creamy white coconut. It's fabulous to plunge into with homemade brandy snaps, spiced with cinnamon.

Preheat the oven to 190°C/375°F/Gas 5.

To make the dips, peel the papaya and place it in a food processor with the lime juice and sugar. Whiz until you have a smooth purée. Transfer to a jug and refrigerate until required. In a separate bowl, whip the coconut cream, yoghurt, sugar and fresh coconut together, transfer to a jug and chill until needed.

For the brandy snaps, place the butter, caster sugar and golden syrup in a small pan and heat gently until everything has melted and the sugar has dissolved. Remove from the heat and add the flour, cinnamon, lemon zest and Grand Marnier liqueur.

Place teaspoonfuls of the mixture spaced well apart on lightly oiled baking sheets and bake for 8–9 minutes until golden brown and set. Remove from the oven and allow to cool for 1 minute. Shape around the lightly oiled handle of a wooden spoon while still warm. If the brandy snaps become too brittle, return to the oven for a few seconds to soften. Allow them to cool completely, and then store in an airtight tin.

To serve, take the jugs of papaya and coconut dips and slowly pour into a large bowl (or 4 smaller individual bowls) at the same time, taking care to keep the 2 dips at opposite sides of the bowl. Swirl the centre with a fork to give a marbled effect.

Serve with the Cinnamon Brandy Snaps.

SERVES 4 (MAKES 20 BRANDY SNAPS)

for the papaya dip

1 ripe but firm papaya (paw paw)
juice 1 lime
2 tbsp caster (superfine) sugar (or to taste)

for the coconut dip

200 ml/7 fl oz/scant 1 cup coconut cream
120 ml/4 fl oz/½ cup Greek yoghurt
2 tbsp caster (superfine) sugar
2 tsp fresh coconut, finely chopped

for the brandy snaps

115 g/4 oz/½ cup butter
115 g/4 oz/½ cup caster (superfine) sugar
2 tbsp golden syrup
90 g/3½ oz/⅔ cup plain (all-purpose) flour, sieved
2 tsp cinnamon
zest 1 lemon
1 tbsp Grand Marnier liqueur

sweet satay dip
with fresh summer fruit sticks

This dip is easy to prepare and is especially popular with children. Even if your guests are not usually great fruit eaters, this fruity dip is sure to win them over.

SERVES 4

for the dip

150 g/5 oz/³/₄ cup chunky peanut butter
200 ml/7 fl oz/scant 1 cup coconut cream
150 ml/5 fl oz/²/₃ cup Greek yoghurt
50 g/2 oz/¹/₄ cup caster (superfine) sugar

for the fruit sticks

assorted ripe fresh fruit such as pineapple, strawberries, plums, peaches, kiwis, apples etc

bamboo satay sticks

To make the dip, place the peanut butter, coconut cream, Greek yoghurt and sugar in a food processor and whiz until everything is nicely combined. Turn into 4 decorative, individual bowls or 1 larger bowl and refrigerate until ready to serve.

Just before serving, wash and prepare a selection of fruit and chop into bite-size chunks. Thread the fruit on to satay sticks.

To serve, place a selection of fruit skewers on 4 small plates and sit the individual bowls of dip alongside. An even more casual way to serve the fruit is to simply arrange it on a large plate in the centre of the table and allow diners to 'stab' their chosen chunks of fruit with cocktail sticks.

passion fruit custard dip
with mango-leather scoops

Fragrant passion fruit has a distinctive
flavour all of its own and a natural affinity
with creamy custard. If the soft, sugary pulp
of a ripe mango is spread out and dried
slowly over several hours, it can be shaped
into pretty scoops just perfect for plunging
into Passion Fruit Custard Dip.

SERVES 4

for the dip

200 ml/7 fl oz/scant 1 cup double (heavy) cream
100 ml/3½ fl oz/scant ½ cup milk
4 egg yolks
50 g/2 oz/¼ cup caster (superfine) sugar
8 passion fruits

for the scoops

2 medium ripe mangoes
1 tbsp caster (superfine) sugar
2 tbsp Malibu liqueur

This recipe is ideally suited to making the day before
serving, to allow for the long cooking time and setting.

To make the dip, pour the double cream and the
milk into a pan and heat until almost boiling.

Meanwhile, put the egg yolk and caster sugar into
a bowl and stir until smooth.

 continued overleaf

Cut the passion fruit in half and scoop out the seeds and juice into a food processor. Whiz for 3 or 4 seconds only (this will loosen the pulp from the seeds, and enable you to extract the maximum amount of juice from each fruit – but any longer could allow a bitter taste to be released from the seeds).

Add the juice to the egg-and-sugar mixture, and stir until smooth. Carefully pour the hot milk on to the egg-and-sugar mixture, stirring constantly. When the mixture is smooth, pour it back into the pan. Stir constantly, over a gentle heat, until the custard is thick enough to leave a clear trail when a finger is drawn along the back of the spoon.

Pour the mixture into 4 ramekins or small individual dessert bowls and leave to chill in the fridge for 2–3 hours until set.

Preheat the oven to 110°C/225°F/Gas ½.

For the scoops, peel the mangoes and put the flesh into the bowl of a food processor. Add the caster sugar and Malibu liqueur and process until you have a thick purée. Line a large, square baking sheet with cling film. Spread the purée over the cling film in a thin but even layer. Place the tray in the oven and leave to dry out for 5–6 hours (depending on how thick your layer of purée is).

Remove the mango leather from the oven and gently peel away the cling film. Cut the leather into strips with scissors and form into scoops or cones. Secure the ends and leave to cool completely.

To serve, set a bowl of dip on each of 4 patterned dessert plates, and place 2 Mango-Leather Scoops to one side.

jelly glazed cointreau dip
with little sticky chocolate cakes

This fluffy dip is laced with Cointreau and topped with a glistening layer of Cointreau and orange jelly.

SERVES 4 (MAKES 24 CAKES)

for the dip

300 ml/10 fl oz/1½ cups double (heavy) cream
zest 2 oranges
75 g/3 oz/¾ cup icing (confectioner's) sugar
5 tbsp Cointreau liqueur
150 ml/5 fl oz/⅔ cup Greek yoghurt
2 tbsp good-quality apricot conserve

for the jelly

1 leaf gelatine
7 tbsp fresh orange juice (about 2 juicy oranges)

4 tbsp Cointreau liqueur
3 tbsp caster (superfine) sugar

for the cakes

65 g/2½ oz/⅓ cup butter
65 g/2½ oz plain chocolate
75 g/3oz/¾ cup icing (confectioner's) sugar
25 g/1 oz/¼ cup plain (all-purpose) flour, sieved
25 g/1 oz/¼ cup ground almonds
2 egg whites

icing sugar to dust

Preheat the oven to 180°C/350°F/Gas 4.

To make the dip, pour the cream into a bowl and add the zest, icing sugar and Cointreau liqueur. Whip to form stiff peaks. Fold in the yoghurt. Sieve the apricot conserve and swirl through the Cointreau mixture. Pour into 4 bowls and refrigerate.

For the jelly, place the gelatine in a bowl and soften with a little cold water. Put the orange juice, Cointreau liqueur and caster sugar into a pan and heat gently until warm. Squeeze the excess water out of the gelatine and stir into the warm Cointreau syrup until dissolved. Pour into a bowl and refrigerate until it begins to set. Pour a layer of jelly over each of the dips. Chill until ready to serve.

For the cakes, place the butter and chocolate in a bowl and melt over a pan of barely simmering water. Add the icing sugar, flour and ground almonds. Whisk the egg whites until they form soft peaks. Take a little of the egg-white mixture and stir this into the chocolate mix, then fold in the rest of the egg white. Leave for 30 minutes or so to firm up. Lightly oil a *petit-four*-size madeleine tin and fill with teaspoonfuls of the mixture. Bake for about 10 minutes, or until firm but springy to the touch. Remove from the oven, dust with a little icing sugar and serve warm with the Jelly Glazed Cointreau Dip.

dollops

From dreamy ice creams to piquant butters,
from vibrant salsas to tangy pestos, from sweet whipped
cream laced with liqueur to creamy potatoes, a simple
dollop of something delicious is an inspired yet
uncomplicated way to lift an everyday dish into
something a little more special.

horseradish potatoes
with char-grilled fillet steaks and candied shallots

These creamy potatoes with a subtle kick of horseradish are perfect with steak and always seem to disappear quickly. It tastes great served with candied shallots and a crisp, green salad.

SERVES 4

for the potatoes

4 large potatoes
175 ml/6 fl oz/½ cup milk
175 ml/6 fl oz/½ cup double (heavy) cream
1 clove garlic, crushed
4–5 tbsp creamed horseradish
 (be quite generous)
salt and freshly ground pepper
40 g/1½ oz/3 tbsp butter

for the shallots

450 g/1 1b shallots
120 ml/4 fl oz/½ cup balsamic vinegar
1 tbsp caster (superfine) sugar
salt and freshly ground black pepper
4 or 5 sprigs fresh thyme
4 tbsp olive oil
4 tbsp water

for the steak

2 tbsp olive oil
salt and freshly ground black pepper
4x 175 g/6 oz fillet steaks

green salad leaves to serve

Preheat the oven to 180°C/350°F/Gas 4.

To make the horseradish potatoes, peel the potatoes and slice very finely (use a food processor or mandolin if you have one). Soak the potato slices in cold water to remove the starch. Meanwhile, put the milk, cream and garlic into a pan and bring to the boil. Remove from the heat and add the creamed horseradish. Taste the mixture, and season with salt and freshly ground black pepper. Remember that potatoes are quite bland, so the mixture needs to taste fairly strong at this point, or the flavour of the horseradish will be lost in the finished dish.

continued overleaf

Brush an ovenproof gratin dish with 15 g/½ oz/1 tbsp of the butter. Drain the potatoes and pat them dry with kitchen paper. Spread a layer of potatoes over the bottom of the dish, season with a little salt and freshly ground black pepper, and drizzle a little of the creamy horseradish mixture over them. Repeat until you have used up all the potatoes and then pour the remaining mixture over the top. Dot with the rest of the butter. Cover with foil and bake for 30–40 minutes until the potatoes are soft and the liquid has been absorbed. Remove the foil and cook for a further 10 minutes until the potatoes are golden brown.

Cook the shallots in the oven at the same time as the potatoes. Cover the shallots with very hot water for 5 minutes or so (this will make peeling them much easier). Drain, then peel them. Put them into a roasting pan and pour over the balsamic vinegar. Sprinkle over the sugar, then season with salt and a little pepper. Dot a few sprigs of thyme here and there. Drizzle over the olive oil and place in the oven. After 30 minutes or so, give them a gentle stir round and add 2 tablespoonfuls of water. Cook for another 10–15 minutes. The shallots should be meltingly soft and caramelized. Remove the thyme before serving.

When you are almost ready to eat, brush a little olive oil over the surface of a griddle pan and place over a high heat until the oil is very hot but not smoking. Place the steaks on the grill for between 2–4 minutes on each side, depending on how you like your steaks cooked (around 2–3 minutes on each side should give you a rare steak, 3 to 4 minutes on each side if you prefer medium – depending on the thickness of your steaks). Remove the steaks from the grill and season with salt and freshly ground black pepper.

Serve the steaks immediately with a green salad and a generous dollop of the Horseradish Potatoes and Candied Shallots.

rustic ham mousse
with fresh pea and celeriac soup

A great way to use up any leftover ham, this mousse makes an ideal topping for all manner of things – and a delectable sandwich filling.

SERVES 4

for the mousse

200 g/7 oz/scant 1 cup cream cheese
150 g/5 oz cooked ham
1 tbsp wholegrain mustard
1 tbsp fresh chives, finely chopped
salt and freshly ground black pepper

for the croutons

2 slices good-quality white bread
1 tbsp olive oil

for the soup

25 g/1 oz/2 tbsp butter
1 large onion
250 g/9 oz celeriac, roughly chopped
450 g/1 lb/4 cups frozen petit pois
900 ml/1½ pt/3½ cups good-quality chicken
  or vegetable stock
1 bay leaf

fresh chives to garnish

Preheat the oven to 200°C/400°F/Gas 6.

To make the mousse, place the cream cheese, ham and mustard together in a food processor, whiz until you have a smooth paste and turn the mixture into a bowl. Stir in the chives and season with salt and freshly ground black pepper. Refrigerate until ready to serve.

For the croutons, cut little circles out of the bread using a small pastry cutter (about 3 cm/1½ in) and brush with a little olive oil. Place on a baking tray and bake for 3–4 minutes until crisp and golden. Remove from the oven and leave to cool.

For the soup, melt the butter in a large pan and gently sauté the onion until softened but not browned. Add the celeriac and continue to cook for a few minutes more. Stir in the peas and pour in the stock. Add the bay leaf. Bring the mixture almost to the boil, then turn down and simmer for about 20–25 minutes until the celeriac is soft when tested with the point of a knife. Remove the bay leaf and transfer to a liquidizer or blender. Blend until smooth and season to taste.

To serve, pour the soup into 4 soup bowls. Place a little Rustic Ham Mousse on each of the croutons and float 3 in the centre of each bowl of soup. Garnish with fresh chives and serve immediately.

chutney from provence
with crisp cheese tarts

This is a delicious chutney to serve with meat, fish or cheese. I often serve it with these little cheese tarts. Made from crisp filo pastry, they are very quick and easy to prepare, and incredibly light.

Preheat the oven to 180°C/350°F/Gas 4.

To make the chutney, place all the ingredients in a large heavy-based pan over a low heat and stir until the sugar has dissolved. Bring to the boil then turn down the heat and simmer for 1–1½ hours, until the vegetables are soft, the liquid has evaporated and the chutney is nice and thick. Cool and store in clean airtight jars until ready to serve.

For the tarts, take 2 squares of filo pastry and lay them at angles to each other to form a star shape. Brush lightly with melted butter and place, butter-side down, in an individual Yorkshire pudding tin, or make nests on an ordinary flat baking sheet. Repeat this with the other squares of pastry. Brush the tops with a little more melted butter. Pop them in the oven and cook for about 3–4 minutes until the nests are light golden brown and crisp.

In a large bowl, mix the 3 cheeses together and add the sun-dried tomatoes. Fold in the fresh basil and season with salt and freshly ground black pepper. Spoon a little of the mixture into each of the filo cases, then return them to the oven for 3–4 minutes, until the cheese is hot and the top is golden brown.

Serve immediately with a generous dollop of the Chutney from Provence.

SERVES 4

for the chutney

2 red onions, coarsely chopped

1 aubergine (eggplant), cut into 2cm/¾ in dice

2 cloves garlic, crushed

3 tomatoes, coarsely chopped

2 courgettes (zucchini), in chunks

2 red (bell) peppers, chopped and tailed then cut into 2 cm/¾ in dice

1 orange (bell) pepper, chopped and tailed then cut into 2 cm/¾ in dice

12 sun-dried tomatoes, quartered

knob fresh ginger, peeled and chopped

7 tbsp water

300 ml/10 fl oz/1½ cups red wine vinegar

150 g/5 oz/¾ cup demerara sugar

1 bay leaf

for the tarts

8 x 15cm/6 in squares filo pastry

50 g/2 oz/¼ cup butter, melted

150 g/5 oz/1¼ cups Gruyère cheese, grated

115 g/4 oz/½ cup mascarpone cheese

75 g/3 oz/1 cup Parmesan cheese, grated

12 sun-dried tomatoes, chopped

8 leaves fresh basil, in small pieces

salt and freshly ground black pepper

tropical fruit salsa
with pepper-crusted tuna steaks

Brimming with exotic flavours and speckled with vibrant colours, a liberal dollop of Tropical Fruit Salsa makes a perfect accompaniment to succulent tuna coated in freshly cracked peppercorns.

SERVES 4

for the salsa

1 small red onion, finely chopped

1 red (bell) pepper, deseeded and cut into 1 cm/½ in dice

1 yellow (bell) pepper, deseeded and cut into 1 cm/½ in dice

1 firm but ripe mango, peeled and cut into 1 cm/½ in dice

1 firm but ripe papaya (paw paw), peeled, deseeded and cut into 1 cm/½ in dice

4 firm, ripe tomatoes, deseeded and finely diced

large bunch fresh coriander (cilantro), finely chopped

juice and zest ½ lime

1 red chilli pepper, deseeded and very finely chopped

½ tsp Tabasco

1 avocado

salt and freshly ground black pepper

for the tuna

2 tbsp fresh cracked black peppercorns

2 tsp dark brown or muscovado sugar

4 × 175 g/6 oz fresh tuna steaks

3 tbsp olive oil

To make the salsa, place the prepared onion, peppers, mango, papaya and diced tomatoes in a large bowl. Add the coriander, lime juice, chilli and Tabasco and give everything a good stir round. If possible, set the mixture to one side for 30 minutes or so to allow the flavours to develop. Just before serving, peel the avocado, remove the stone and cut into cubes as for the other ingredients. Stir it into the salsa and season to taste with salt and freshly ground black pepper.

Prepare the peppercorns using a pestle and mortar or a rolling pin – just roll over them until they crack into small but defined pieces.

For the tuna, combine the cracked peppercorns and muscovado sugar in a bowl, then press the mixture firmly on to both sides of each tuna steak. Heat the olive oil in a frying pan or skillet and add the tuna steaks. Cook over a high heat for about 2 to 3 minutes on each side, depending on thickness.

To serve, place a pepper-crusted tuna steak on each of 4 dinner plates. Top with a generous dollop of Tropical Fruit Salsa and serve immediately.

chinese-style salsa
with soy-glazed salmon

Piquant and fruity, with a gentle nip of stem ginger, this salsa lends an extra oriental touch to soy-glazed salmon. If you can't obtain any plum seasoning, use rice wine vinegar instead.

SERVES 4

for the salsa

4 firm but ripe red plums, halved, stoned and diced
1 small red onion, finely chopped
1 orange (bell) pepper, topped, tailed and diced
4 knobs stem ginger, finely chopped
1 tbsp sesame seeds
1 stalk lemon grass
8–10 mint leaves, finely chopped
1 tbsp fresh coriander (cilantro), finely chopped
2 tbsp Japanese ume plum seasoning
salt and freshly ground black pepper

for the salmon

1 tbsp Indonesian sweet soy sauce (ketjap manis)
1 tbsp honey
juice ½ lime
4 × 175 g/6 oz salmon fillets, skinned and pinboned (use a pair of tweezers to remove the tiny pinbones from the fillets)

To make the salsa, place the plums, onion, pepper, ginger and sesame seeds in a large bowl. Remove the tough outer leaves of the lemon grass and, using the blunt handle of a knife, bash it along its length and chop it very finely. Add this to the bowl, with the mint and coriander. Finally, add the plum seasoning and season with salt and freshly ground black pepper. Set aside.

For the salmon, mix the soy sauce, honey and lime juice together and brush liberally over the salmon. Cook under a hot grill until the top is caramelised and the salmon is cooked through but slightly opaque in the centre (about 5–6 minutes, depending on the thickness of the salmon).

Serve immediately with the Chinese-style salsa.

fresh basil pesto

with chèvre toasties and popped tomatoe

SERVES 4

for the pesto

2 very large handfuls of basil
 leaves

50 g/2 oz/²⁄₃ cup Parmesan,
 grated

50 g/2 oz/¹⁄₂ cup pine nuts

2 cloves garlic, crushed

1 tbsp fresh lemon juice

4 tbsp olive oil

for the tomatoes

450 g/1 lb cherry tomatoes

1 clove garlic, crushed

1 tsp sugar

1 tbsp balsamic vinegar

2 tbsp olive oil

salt and freshly ground black
 pepper

for the toasties

4 slices good-quality white
 bread

2 tbsp olive oil

1 tsp thyme leaves, finely
 chopped

2 tbsp Black Olive Tapenade (see
 page 28)

4 × 90 g/3½ oz slices chèvre log

8 long lengths chives to garnish
 (optional)

Fragrant basil pesto is quick and easy to make, especially if you use a food processor, and the flavours are much more lively and intense than the shop-bought variety. Pesto is delicious served with these tasty Chèvre (goat's cheese) Toasties and plump little cherry tomatoes.

Preheat the oven to 200°C/400°F/Gas 6.

To make the pesto, place the basil, Parmesan, pine nuts, garlic and lemon juice in a food processor. Whiz to combine. Add the olive oil until you have a lightly textured paste. Store in a screw-top jar and chill until ready to serve.

Wash the tomatoes and place in an ovenproof dish. Sprinkle over the garlic and sugar. Dribble over balsamic vinegar and olive oil. Season with a little salt and freshly ground black pepper. Place in a hot oven for 8–10 minutes until the skins begin to pop and the juices are released. Remove from the oven and keep warm.

For the toasties, cut 2 circles from each slice of bread, using a pastry cutter just slightly larger than the cheese rounds. Brush with olive oil and scatter with a few finely chopped thyme leaves. Bake for about 5 minutes until light golden and crisp. Remove from the oven. Spread a little tapenade on to one side of each toast circle, then sandwich the circles in pairs with a slice of cheese as filling. Return to the oven for a few minutes, until the cheese has softened slightly. For extra effect, tie 2 long lengths of chive around each sandwich and knot at the top.

Serve at once with the pesto and warm tomatoes.

lemon aïoli
with roast sea trout and young summer vegetables

My lemon version of traditional garlic mayonnaise is perfect for summer entertaining when friends or family get together in the sunshine. A light olive oil is best for the mayonnaise, although equal quantities of olive oil mixed with sunflower oil make a good alternative.

SERVES 6–8

for the mayonnaise

1 egg
zest 2 lemons (unwaxed if possible)
1 tsp Dijon mustard
4 cloves garlic, crushed
300 ml/10 fl oz /1½ cups light olive oil
juice 1 lemon
salt and freshly ground black pepper

for the fish

1 whole sea trout (about 1.8 kg/4 lb), head removed, gutted and cleaned (ask your fishmonger to do this for you)

1 large onion, sliced thinly
1 lemon, sliced (use the zest for the mayonnaise)
1 bunch flat-leaf parsley
120 ml/4 fl oz/½ cup dry white wine
675 g/1½ lb new potatoes, steamed or boiled in salted water until tender

675 g/1½ lb small young carrots, lightly cooked
450 g /1lb green beans, lightly cooked
450 g /1 lb sugar-snap peas, washed but uncooked
1 medium cauliflower, cut into florets and lightly cooked
1 small head broccoli, cut into florets and lightly cooked
6 eggs, hard-boiled, shelled and quartered
6 small raw beetroot, wrapped in foil and roasted for 30 minutes in the oven
6 plum tomatoes, quartered
24 black olives

freshly chopped parsley to garnish

Preheat the oven to 200°C/400°F/Gas 6.

To make the mayonnaise, place the egg, lemon zest, mustard, garlic and a pinch of salt in the bowl of a blender. Whiz to combine. With the motor running, begin to trickle in the olive oil slowly until you have added about a third, and then you can add the remaining oil more quickly. When all the oil has been incorporated, add the lemon juice and adjust the seasoning, adding a little more salt if necessary, and a little freshly ground black pepper. Whiz again to blend. Place the mayonnaise in a beautiful bowl, cover and refrigerate.

To cook the trout, brush a large piece of turkey foil with olive oil and lay it on the bottom of a roasting tin. Pop the trout on to the foil. Place a row of onions along the inside of the fish cavity and top with a row of lemon slices and some sprigs of parsley. Pour over the wine and sprinkle with a little sea salt. Loosely close up the foil and crimp the edges tightly. Place in the oven and cook for around 35 minutes (8–10 minutes per 450g/1lb). Take care with timing, as fish is easily overcooked and this will impair the delicate texture and flavour. When the trout is cooked, the flesh should part easily when tested with the tip of a sharp knife. Open the foil parcel, but leave the fish to cool in the juices.

When the trout has cooled, lift it out on to a large piece of greaseproof paper or baking parchment. Carefully peel away the skin on the uppermost side and gently scrape away any dark flesh. Lifting up the edges of the paper transfer the trout to a large serving platter, with the remaining skin now uppermost. Remove the skin and dark flesh from this side, as before. Arrange the vegetables and eggs around the trout, and garnish with a scattering of freshly chopped parsley.

Serve at room temperature with the Lemon Aïoli.

preserved lemon and stem ginger yoghurt
with volcano chicken

This tangy yoghurt is bursting with lively citrus notes and offers a beautiful contrast to strongly flavoured or spicy foods. Try it with hot, sizzling Volcano Chicken, and allow your tastebuds to erupt.

SERVES 4

for the yoghurt

300 ml/10 fl oz/1½ cups thick Greek yoghurt
½ preserved lemon (see Larder Basics
 page 10), flesh removed and the peel
 finely chopped
1 spring onion, very finely chopped
1 tbsp chopped mint, finely chopped
2 knobs stem ginger, finely chopped

for the chicken

2 tbsp olive oil
8 plump free-range chicken thighs
1 or 2 fresh chillies, deseeded and chopped
7 tbsp Indonesian sweet soy sauce
 (ketjap manis)
4 tbsp good-quality chicken stock

plain steamed rice to serve

Preheat the oven to 190°C/375°F/Gas 5.

To make the yoghurt, combine all the ingredients in a bowl, stir well and refrigerate until required.

for the chicken, heat the olive oil in a frying pan and fry the chicken thighs for a few minutes until golden brown all over. Remove them from the pan and place them in an ovenproof dish, so that the thighs fit snugly together. Sprinkle the chopped chillies evenly over the chicken. Mix the soy sauce and the stock together and pour this over the chicken thighs. Cook in the oven for 40–50 minutes, turning from time to time, until the chicken is dark and glazed and the sauce has bubbled down and thickened.

Serve the Volcano Chicken with some plain steamed rice, pour over the sauce and serve with a generous dollop of Preserved Lemon and Stem Ginger Yoghurt.

raspberry, rosemary and macadamia pesto
with smoked venison and melon salad

This fruity pesto offers a terrific contrast to tender, smoky venison, and partnered with sweet ripe melon makes an unusual and delightful dinner party starter or light lunch. Try combining it with other smoked meats, too.

SERVES 4

for the pesto

90 g/3½ oz macadamia or cashew nuts

20 g/¾ oz/1½ tbsp butter, melted

4 juniper berries, crushed

1 stalk lemon grass

1 tbsp fresh rosemary, finely chopped

2 tsp fresh young sage, finely chopped

2 tsp raspberry vinegar

2-3 tsp caster (superfine) sugar

90 g/3½ oz/½ cup fresh raspberries

salt and freshly ground black pepper

2 tbsp olive oil

115g/4 oz smoked venison, sliced wafer thin

½ ripe but firm melon

Preheat the oven to 180°C/350°F/Gas 4.

To make the pesto, toss the nuts in the melted butter, place them on a baking sheet and roast in the oven for 4–5 minutes until golden brown. Leave to cool, then roughly chop them and place in a bowl with the crushed juniper berries.

Remove the tougher outer leaves from the lemon grass, bash it along its length with the handle of a large knife, then chop very finely and add to the nut mixture. Stir in the chopped rosemary and sage, followed by the vinegar and sugar. Make sure you use young sage leaves as they can become slightly bitter with age. Carefully add the raspberries, crushing them gently but leaving the mixture nicely textured with some fairly large pieces here and there. Season to taste with salt and plenty of freshly ground black pepper. Drizzle over the olive oil and fold in gently.

For the venison and melon salad, arrange the smoked venison on individual plates or 1 large, splendid serving plate. Using a vegetable peeler, cut ribbons of melon and arrange them nicely with the venison.

Serve with a generous dollop of the Raspberry, Rosemary and Macadamia Pesto.

smooshy corn
with parmesan crusted cod

I can hear you asking, 'What on earth is Smooshy Corn?' Being a Yorkshire lass, I still have a soft spot for the comforting soft, green mass of mushy peas that always accompanied fish and chips in my early years. So this is my compromise, a squishy-sweet dollop of bay-scented, buttery corn set atop tasty cod with a tangy Parmesan crust.

SERVES 4

for the corn

350 g/12 oz/2 cups frozen sweetcorn, defrosted

1 fresh bay leaf

pinch sugar

40g/1½oz/3 tbsp butter

salt and freshly ground black pepper

for the cod

150 g/5 oz/2½ cups fresh breadcrumbs

50 g/2 oz/⅔ cup Parmesan, finely grated

1 clove garlic, crushed

1 tbsp chives, finely chopped

1 egg white

4 × 175 g/6 oz fresh cod fillets, skinned and pinboned (use a pair of tweezers to remove the tiny pinbones from the fillets)

oil for frying

To make the corn, put the sweetcorn and bay leaf into a pan and add enough water to barely cover. Bring to the boil, turn down the heat and simmer for 3–4 minutes. Drain well and place in a food processor with a pinch of sugar. Whiz until you have a smooth purée. Leave to cool a little, then add the butter. Whiz again until thoroughly blended, and season well with salt and freshly ground black pepper. Set aside but keep warm.

Meanwhile, prepare the cod. Place the breadcrumbs, Parmesan, garlic and chives together in a large bowl and season well with salt and freshly ground black pepper. Whisk the egg white very lightly with a fork. Dip the cod pieces into the egg white and then coat with the breadcrumb mix, taking care to get a nice thick layer all round each piece of fish. Heat the oil in a frying pan and fry the fish for about 4–5 minutes on each side until the batter is golden brown and crisp and the fish is cooked through (exact timing will depend on the thickness of the fish). Remove from the pan and drain on kitchen paper.

Serve the Parmesan Crusted Cod immediately with a big dollop of Smooshy Corn.

red pepper and pink peppercorn butter
with char-grilled swordfish

Flavoured butters are so versatile and this pale golden version, speckled through with red peppers and pink peppercorns and freckled with fresh green parsley, looks as good as it tastes.

SERVES 4

for the butter

2 tbsp pink peppercorns
150 g/5 oz/1½ sticks
  butter, softened
½ red (bell) pepper, finely diced
1 tbsp wholegrain mustard
1 tbsp flat leaf parsley,
  finely chopped

salt and freshly ground
  black pepper

for the fish

2 tbsp olive oil
4 swordfish steaks
juice ½ lemon

To make the butter, roughly crush the pink peppercorns with a pestle and mortar. Whisk the softened butter slightly to lighten, then add the peppercorns, red pepper, mustard and parsley. Beat well to combine. Turn out into a bowl and set aside until required.

For the fish, heat a griddle pan and brush with a little olive oil. When the pan is hot, place the swordfish steaks on it and cook for 3–4 minutes on each side depending on the thickness of the steaks. Try not to disturb the fish too much while cooking so that you achieve an attractive striped look! Remove from the griddle and add a little lemon and some salt.

Serve whilst piping hot, with the Red Pepper and Pink Peppercorn butter.

vanilla spiced mascarpone
with warm fat rascals
and bay scented figs

Mascarpone is a thick, creamy soft cheese from Italy. When sweetened very lightly and freckled with the tiny, black seeds from fat Madagascan vanilla pods, the flavour is sublime. Delicious with a fresh fruit salad or crisp apple tart, I love to combine it with warm Fat Rascals – traditional Yorkshire cakes that are a cross between a scone and a rock cake.

SERVES 4

for the cheese cream

250 g/9 oz/1 cup mascarpone cheese
2 tbsp milk
25 g/1 oz/2 tbsp caster (superfine) sugar
1 plump, fresh vanilla pod

for the cakes

150 g/5 oz/1¼ cups plain (all-purpose) flour, sieved
150 g/5 oz/1¼ cups self-raising (self-rising) flour
1 tsp baking powder
130 g/4½ oz/²⁄₃ cup butter
90 g/3½ oz/7 tbsp golden caster (superfine) sugar
zest 1 orange
zest 1 lemon
1 tsp ground cinnamon
½ tsp grated nutmeg

150 g/5 oz/scant 1 cup mixed dried fruits (I use raisins, currants and sultanas in roughly equal amounts)
1 egg, lightly beaten
2–3 tbsp milk
1 egg yolk
1 tbsp water
pinch salt

cherries and whole peeled almonds to decorate

for the figs

200 ml/7 fl oz/scant 1 cup water
200 g/7 oz/1 cup caster (superfine) sugar
1–2 fresh bay leaves
6 firm but ripe fresh figs

Preheat the oven to 200°C/400°F/Gas 6.

To make the cheese cream, put the mascarpone, milk and caster sugar into a bowl. Using a small, sharp knife, carefully cut down along the length of the vanilla pod. Scrape out the seeds and pop them into the bowl with the rest of the ingredients. (Keep the vanilla pod and add it to a jar of sugar. The sugar will absorb the delicious vanilla notes and is lovely sprinkled and stirred into all manner of things!)

For the cakes, sieve both flours and the baking powder into a large bowl. Add the butter and, using your fingers, rub it into the flour until the mixture resembles fine breadcrumbs. Add the sugar, orange zest and lemon zest, spices and dried fruit. Stir thoroughly until everything is well combined. Add the egg and enough milk to bring the mixture together into a soft dough. Form into 6 rounds about 2 cm/½ in deep. Mix the egg yolk, water and salt together and brush over the Fat Rascals to glaze them. Place 2 half-cherries on each, for eyes, and 3 almonds for teeth. Place on an oven tray and bake for about 15–20 minutes, until golden brown and firm. Set out on to a rack to cool slightly.

Fat Rascals are best when served warm from the oven, but they freeze well, and once defrosted will reheat beautifully in a low oven.

For the figs, put the water and sugar into a pan and heat gently until the sugar melts. Add the bay leaves. Bring the syrup up to boil and simmer for 2–3 minutes. Carefully wash each fig and cut in half. Place them, cut-side down, in a shallow dish. Pour the hot syrup over the figs, then set aside to cool. As the syrup cools, the bay leaves will impart a delicate flavour to the figs, but the figs will retain their shape.

To serve, cut open a Warm Fat Rascal and top with some Vanilla Spiced Mascarpone and the Bay Scented Figs.

blueberry cheescakes
with rosemary and orange brioche

Who would imagine that slices of oven-crisped brioche, some fat little blueberries and a dollop of cream cheese could make a stunning dessert in no time at all? Once you have tried these quick little cheesecakes they are sure to become a favourite.

SERVES 4

for the butter

1 tbsp fresh rosemary, very finely chopped

zest 1 orange

50 g/2 oz/¼ cup butter

4 rounds brioche of about 6 cm/
  2½ in diameter

1 tbsp caster (superfine) sugar

for the cheesecakes

7 tbsp water

50 g/2 oz/¼ cup caster (superfine) sugar

375 g/13 oz/3¼ cups fresh blueberries

300 g/11 oz/scant 1½ cups cream cheese

1 tsp vanilla extract

mint sprigs to garnish (optional)

Preheat the oven to 190°/375°/Gas 5.

To make the butter, blend the rosemary and orange zest evenly into the butter. Spread the butter over the brioche rounds and sprinkle a little sugar over each. Place them in the oven and bake for 5 minutes or so until golden brown. Remove from the oven and set aside – they will crisp as they cool.

For the cheesecakes, put the water and sugar in a small pan. Bring to the boil and bubble gently for a couple of minutes. Add half of the blueberries and simmer over a low heat for about 3 minutes, until the blueberries have popped and begun to turn syrupy. Remove from the heat and cool for a couple of minutes. Add the remaining blueberries and stir – the heat should soften them, but they should remain whole. Remove from the heat and allow to cool completely.

Whip the cream cheese with the vanilla extract until fluffy. Take the brioche rounds and place 1 on each of 4 dainty dessert plates. Spoon a small dollop of the cream cheese mixture on each brioche round and top with a few of the blueberries lifted out of the syrup. Then place a good-sized dollop of the cream cheese carefully on top. Arrange the remaining blueberries and syrup over and around the cheesecakes. Garnish each with a sprig of mint and serve immediately.

espresso jelly
with iced chestnut terrine

Sweet espresso is spiked with coffee liqueur, set to a jelly and served with a rich iced chestnut terrine – truly delicious.

SERVES 4

for the jelly

2½ leaves gelatine
300 ml/10 fl oz/1¼ cup strong hot coffee
3 tbsp caster (superfine) sugar
4 tbsp Kahlua liqueur

for the terrine

550 ml/18 fl oz/2½ cups double (heavy) cream

1 x 200 g/7 oz/small can sweetened chestnut purée
5 tbsp Armagnac brandy
3 egg whites
1 tbsp caster (superfine) sugar
75 g/3 oz marrons glacés (candied chestnuts), chopped
75 g/3 oz plain chocolate

You will need a 1.2 litre /2 pt/5 cup terrine mould or loaf tin, lined with cling film

To make the jelly, soak the gelatine in a little cold water to soften. Pour the coffee into a bowl and stir in the sugar and the Kahlua liqueur. Squeeze the excess water out of the gelatine and add to the coffee mixture. Stir thoroughly until the gelatine has completely dissolved and place in the fridge to set.

For the terrine, put the double cream, chestnut purée and Armagnac into a food processor and whiz until completely blended, scraping down the bowl until the mixture has thickened slightly. Whisk the egg whites and caster sugar until stiff. Fold a little of the egg white into the chestnut-cream mixture to loosen it, then carefully fold in the rest, keeping the mixture light. Fold in the marrons glacés. Turn the mixture into the prepared tin and place in the freezer to set.

Put the chocolate into a clean food processor and chop very finely. Remove the frozen terrine from the freezer, release it from the mould and trim to create a log shape. Sprinkle the chocolate over the top and sides, pressing it in lightly to coat them, but leaving the ends free. Return to the freezer until ready to serve.

To serve, cut the terrine into thin slices and place in the centre of elegant dessert plates with a generous dollop of Espresso Jelly on top.

cheesy lemon fluff
with Nana May's butterfly cakes

Among the most vivid memories I have of my childhood are teatime visits to my Nana May's. The house was always full of people, and the table brimming with the lightest, largest butterfly cakes in the world. I can't seem to get exactly the same taste that I remember, but this simple fluffy cheesy-lemon topping has now become the favourite when I have visitors for tea.

MAKES/SERVES 12

for the fluff

200 g/7 oz/scant 1 cup cream cheese

2 generous tbsp good-quality lemon curd

for the cakes

115 g/4 oz/¹⁄₂ cup butter, softened

115 g/4 oz/¹⁄₂ cup caster (superfine) sugar

2 eggs, beaten

1 tsp vanilla extract

175 g/6 oz/1¹⁄₂ cups plain (all-purpose) flour, sieved

2 tbsp baking powder

5 tbsp milk

You will need paper cake cases

Preheat the oven to 180°C/350°F/Gas 4.

To make the fluff, beat the cream cheese and lemon curd in a bowl until light and fluffy. Refrigerate until required.

For the cakes, beat the butter and sugar together until light and fluffy, using a wooden spoon. Gradually add the eggs and vanilla extract and stir until the mixture is smooth. Fold in the flour and baking powder and add the milk. Divide the mixture between 12 fairy-cake cases and cook for about 20 minutes until golden brown, well risen and springy to the touch. Leave to cool completely, then slice off the tops and reserve. Top each cake with a good spoonful of the Cheesy Lemon Fluff.

To serve, cut the little pieces of reserved cake in half and place them back on the cakes to resemble butterfly wings. Dust with icing sugar and serve.

mascarpone sorbet
with cherry frangipane tart

Freshly churned mascarpone sorbet is one of my favourite ices and it's so easy to make in an ice cream maker. With its smooth, dreamy texture, a lavish dollop marries well with a host of different desserts. Here I've teamed it with a lovely fresh cherry tart.

Preheat the oven to 180°C/350°F/Gas 4.

To make the sorbet, place the water and caster sugar in a pan and heat gently until the sugar has dissolved. Add the milk. Put the mascarpone into a food processor and add the milk mixture. Whiz until fully combined. Freeze in an ice cream machine.

Meanwhile, make the pastry for the tart. Put the butter and caster sugar into a food processor and whiz until you have a smooth mixture, scraping down the sides from time to time. Add the egg yolk and process again. Add the flour and whiz briefly until the mixture begins to clump together. Stop the machine and scrape down the sides of the bowl. Whiz briefly once more. Stop the machine and form the pastry into a ball. Cover in cling film and place in the fridge for 30 minutes.

Roll the pastry out to fit the tin. Chill for 30 minutes. Prick the pastry shell and bake it blind (without any filling) for 10–15 minutes until light golden. Cool.

For the filling, place the ground almonds, butter and caster sugar in the food processor and whiz until smooth. Add the eggs and whiz again. Pour into the pastry case and arrange the cherries on top. Cook for 30 minutes until golden brown and set. Remove from the oven and cool.

Dust the top of the tart with icing sugar and serve with Mascarpone Sorbet.

SERVES 4

for the sorbet

200 ml/7 fl oz/scant 1 cup water
90 g/3½ oz/7 tbsp caster (superfine) sugar
200 ml/7 fl oz/scant 1 cup milk
500 g/1¼ lb/2 cups mascarpone cheese

for the pastry

175 g/6 oz/¾ cup butter
50 g/2 oz/¼ cup caster (superfine) sugar
1 egg yolk
250 g/9 oz/2½ cups plain (all-purpose) flour, sieved

for the filling

90 g/3½ oz/¾ cup ground almonds
90 g/3½ oz/7 tbsp butter
90 g/3½ oz/7 tbsp caster (superfine) sugar
2 eggs
250 g/9 oz fresh cherries, pitted
icing (confectioner's) sugar to dust

You will need a 20 cm/8 in loose-bottomed tart tin

stem ginger and pesto
with honey-baked apples

Stem ginger, dark sticky molasses sugar and toasted walnuts were
made for each other and make natural partners for a sublime sweet
pesto. A generous dollop atop a honey-baked apple creates a delicious
dessert that has a regular place in my winter-dessert repertoire.

SERVES 4

for the pesto

2 tbsp dark molasses sugar

6 knobs stem ginger

6 tbsp stem ginger syrup

zest 1 orange

115 g/4 oz/1 cup walnuts, lightly toasted

½ tsp ground cinnamon

for the apples

4 crisp dessert apples, such as Granny Smith
  or Braeburn

2 tbsp lemon juice

2 tbsp thick honey

40 g/1½ oz/3 tbsp butter, melted

chilled Greek yoghurt to serve

Preheat the oven to 200°C/400°F/Gas 6.

To make the pesto, place the sugar, stem ginger and its syrup in a food
processor and whiz until smooth. Add the orange zest and whiz again briefly. Add
the walnuts and process until you have a coarsely textured paste. Transfer to a
bowl, stir in the cinnamon and set aside.

Wash the apples and cut a medium-thick slice from the top of each, leaving
the stalk intact if possible. Remove the central core from the main part of each
apple and drizzle over the lemon juice, honey and butter. Place the apples in
a shallow dish, pour in 4–5 tablespoonfuls of cold water and bake until the apples
are soft throughout when tested with the point of a skewer (40–50 minutes
depending on the size and ripeness of the apples). Check regularly and baste with
any juices that have collected in the dish.

Serve hot with the pesto and a good dollop of Greek yoghurt.

grand marnier cream
with little ginger puddings

Grand Marnier liqueur makes a sumptuous combination with these little ginger puddings. Try to use unsulphured dried apricots as they have a distinguished dark colour and distinct flavour.

MAKES 6 PUDDINGS

for the cream

300 ml/10 fl oz/1½ cups fresh double (heavy) cream
4 tbsp Grand Marnier liqueur
zest 1 orange
2 tbsp caster (superfine) sugar

for the puddings

75 g/3 oz/½ cup dried apricots
2 tbsp brandy
115 g/4 oz/½ cup butter

115 g/4 oz/½ cup muscovado sugar
3 pieces stem ginger, finely chopped
2 eggs, beaten
1 tsp ground ginger
1 tsp ground cinnamon
115 g/4 oz/1 cup self-raising (self-rising) flour, sieved
½ tsp bicarbonate of soda
50 g/2 oz/½ cup walnuts, toasted and chopped
6 tbsp stem ginger syrup

You will need 6 × 150 ml/5 fl oz/⅔ cup metal pudding basins or ramekins, greased with a little butter

Preheat the oven to 180°C/350°F/Gas 4.

To make the cream, pour the cream into a large bowl and add the Grand Marnier liqueur, orange zest and sugar. Whip until the mixture forms soft peaks. Cover and refrigerate until required.

For the puddings, cut the dried apricots into small pieces, pour over the brandy and leave to soak for 30 minutes. Place the butter and sugar in a pan and heat gently until melted. Turn the mixture into a large bowl and stir in the chopped stem ginger, beaten eggs, ground ginger and cinnamon. Add the flour and bicarbonate of soda and stir well. Fold in the dried apricots, brandy and walnuts.

Fill the pudding basins about three-quarters full with the mixture, then place them on a baking tray. Bake for 25–30 minutes, until the puddings are risen and firm . Cool for several minutes, then turn out on to individual serving plates.

Drizzle a generous tablespoon of stem ginger syrup over each pudding and serve with a liberal dollop of Grand Marnier Cream.

fresh lemon sherbet
with brioche `n` berry tumble

Lemon sherbet is bursting with citrus flavour. Serve it with this blissful, easy-to-make summer berry dessert for a magical combination.

SERVES 4

for the sherbet

550 ml/18 fl oz/2½ cups Greek yoghurt
90 g/3½ oz/7 tbsp icing (confectioner's) sugar
7 tbsp lemon juice
50 ml/2 fl oz/¼ cup water
zest 2 lemons

for the sugar syrup

7 tbsp water
75 g/3 oz/scant ½ cup caster (superfine) sugar

for the tumble

1 kg/2¼ lb 4oz mixed summer berries
4 tbsp Framboise liqueur
200 g/7 oz brioche, cut into largish chunks

A handful fresh raspberries, strawberries or redcurrants and mint sprigs to garnish

You will need an ice cream machine

To make the sherbet, pour the Greek yoghurt into a large bowl with the icing sugar, lemon juice, water and lemon zest. Stir well and freeze in an ice cream machine.

For the sugar syrup, place the water and sugar in a small saucepan over a low heat and stir until dissolved. Turn the heat up and bubble for 2 minutes. Remove from the heat and set aside.

For the tumble, place the berries in a large saucepan. Pour over the sugar syrup. Simmer gently for 3–4 minutes, until the fruit has softened *very* slightly and released lots of juice. Remove from the heat and add the Framboise liqueur. Leave until completely cold. (During winter I often use frozen berries. I allow them to defrost, add the liqueur and sugar then proceed from the point at which the cooked berries are cooled.)

Drain the excess juice from the fruits into another bowl. Take 4 dessert dishes and place a generous spoonful of fruit into the bottom of each. Soak the chunks of brioche in the juices and place a spoonful of juice-soaked brioche into each dish on top of the fruit. Repeat the layers once more. Finish with a layer of fruit.

Garnish with a few fresh raspberries, strawberries or redcurrants and a sprig of mint and serve with Fresh Lemon Sherbet.

amaretto and lemon cream
with caramel crunch peaches

I love sweet, rich almondy liqueurs, and when my parents lived in Portugal for a number of years I became quite partial to the Portuguese liqueur Ameginha. The Portuguese often serve it in liqueur glasses with a squeeze of fresh lemon juice floating on the top. This lovely combination of lemon and liqueur gives a real flourish to fresh double cream and will add a special touch to a range of different desserts, but fresh summer peaches with a crunchy caramel coating are particularly good.

SERVES 4

for the cream

300 ml/10 fl oz/1¼ cups double (heavy) cream

zest 1 lemon

2 tbsp lemon juice

4 tbsp icing sugar, sieved

4 tbsp Amaretto liqueur

for the peaches

4 large ripe but firm peaches

40 g/1½ oz/3 tbsp butter

4–5 tbsp demerara sugar

fresh mint to garnish

To make the cream, place the double cream in a large bowl and add the lemon zest and juice, icing sugar and Amaretto liqueur. Using a balloon whisk, stir everything round until well mixed, check that the sweetness is to your liking, then whip until the mixture holds soft peaks. Refrigerate until required.

Cut the peaches in half from top to bottom and twist gently apart. Carefully remove the stone with the point of a sharp knife. Melt the butter over a medium heat. Dip the cut surfaces of each half-peach firmly into the demerara sugar then place the peach halves sugar-side down in the hot butter. Cook for 3–4 minutes until the cut surface has caramelized and formed a crunchy coating. Remove from the pan and place 2 peach halves on each of 4 decorative dessert plates.

Serve with a generous dollop of Amaretto and Lemon Cream and garnish with fresh mint.

apricot and vanilla butter
with spiced apple and mincemeat tart

Dark, unsulphured dried apricots have a fabulous deep flavour and I have used them here to make a luscious creamy butter.

SERVES 4

for the butter

150 g/5 oz/1¼ sticks butter, softened
250 g/9 oz/1½ cups dried apricots
1 tbsp caster (superfine) sugar
1 tsp vanilla extract

for the tart

175 g/6 oz/¾ cup butter
50 g/2 oz/½ cup caster (superfine) sugar
1 egg yolk

250 g/9 oz/2½ cups plain (all-purpose) flour, sieved

for the filling

5 crisp eating apples
25 g/1 oz/2 tbsp butter
2 tbsp Calvados brandy
400 g/14 oz/1¼ cups good-quality mincemeat
25 g/1 oz/¼ cup ground almonds
50 g/2 oz/½ cup flaked almonds

You will need a 20 cm/8 in loose-bottomed tart tin

Preheat the oven to 180°C/350°F/Gas 4.

To make the butter, place all the ingredients in a food processor and whiz to combine. Turn out into a bowl and refrigerate to firm up until required.

For the pastry, place the butter and sugar in a food processor and whiz until smooth. Add the egg yolk and process again, scraping down the sides a couple of times as you go. Add the flour and whiz to combine, then gather up the pastry into a ball. Wrap it in cling film and leave in the fridge for an hour or so.

Roll the pastry out to fit the tin, then bake blind (prick the pastry case all over with a fork and bake it without the filling) for 10–15 minutes until light golden and crisp. Remove from the oven and leave to cool.

For the filling, peel and core the apples. Chop into 1 cm/½ in chunks. Melt the butter, then add the apples. Sauté the apples until soft. Add the Calvados and set it alight. When the flames subside, continue to cook for 2–3 minutes until some of the liquid has evaporated. Stir in the mincemeat. Sprinkle the ground almonds over the part-cooked pastry case and fill with the mincemeat mixture. Scatter over the flaked almonds, then bake until golden brown.

Serve warm with the Apricot and Vanilla Butter.

candied kumquats
with dark chocolate marquise

for the kumquats

300 g/11 oz fresh kumquats

for the syrup

150 ml/5 fl oz/²/₃ cup water
90 g/3½ oz/7 tbsp cup caster
  (superfine) sugar
juice 2 oranges

for the marquise

175 g/6 oz good-quality dark
  chocolate
115 g/4 oz/½ cup butter, diced
2 egg yolks
4 tbsp Kahlua liqueur
4 tbsp caster (superfine) sugar
1 tbsp liquid glucose
2½ tbsp cocoa powder
zest 2 oranges
120 ml/4 fl oz/½ cup double
  (heavy) cream
200g/7oz/scant 1 cup
  mascarpone

You will need a small loaf tin or
terrine mould approximately
750 ml/1½ pt/3 cups in
capacity, lined with cling film

Candied kumquats have a beautiful flavour
and a deep orange sparkle, and they make a
stunning combination served with Dark
Chocolate Marquise (a rich mousse),
although I often serve them as a fruity
topping for creamy ices such as Mascarpone
Sorbet (see page 75) or rich vanilla ice cream.

To prepare the kumquats, wash the kumquats and
cut them in half. Remove the pips and place them in
a pan. Cover them with cold water and bring to the
boil. Simmer gently for 10 minutes to remove the
bitterness from the skin. Drain and then refresh in
cold water. For the syrup, place the water, caster
sugar and orange juice in a pan and bring to the
boil. Turn down the heat and add the kumquats.
Simmer for 25–30 minutes until the kumquats are
soft and translucent and the syrup has thickened.
Leave to cool.

For the marquise, melt the chocolate in a large
bowl over a pan of barely simmering water. Remove
from the heat and add the diced butter. Stir well to
mix, then leave to cool. Place the eggs, Kahlua
liqueur, sugar, glucose, cocoa powder and orange
zest in the bowl of a food processor with the cooled
chocolate mixture and whiz until smooth. Add the
cream and mascarpone and whiz again, scraping
down the sides of the bowl to make sure that
everything is well mixed and smooth.

Pour the mixture into the lined tin or mould. Chill in
the fridge for several hours (or overnight) until firm.

Serve in thin slices with the Candied Kumquats.

drizzles

A drizzle of something quite simple can offer the

perfect alternative to a heavy or complicated sauce.

Light, easily prepared and brimming with fresh flavours,

the recipes that follow make up a selection of

interchangeable drizzles and dishes that will

complement each other beautifully.

sticky pomegranate and wild apricot drizzle
with honey-glazed duck breasts

Pomegranate molasses are dark and sticky
with an intriguing sour-sweet flavour, and
are now quite widely available. They make a
lovely drizzle when combined with sweet
wild apricots and tangy Worcester sauce –
perfect with honey-glazed duck breasts.

SERVES 4

for the drizzle

3 shallots, peeled and finely chopped

2 cloves garlic, crushed

7 tbsp olive oil

90 g/3½ oz/½ cup dried apricots (use the unsulphured type if
you can find them)

2 tbsp pomegranate molasses

4 tbsp Worcester sauce

1 tbsp honey

7 tbsp good-quality chicken stock

for the duck

4 duck breasts

2 tbsp honey

salt and freshly ground pepper

seeds from 1 fresh pomegranate to garnish

continued overleaf

Preheat the oven to 200°C/400°F/Gas 6.

To make the drizzle, sauté the shallots and garlic gently in 2 tbsp oil until softened but not browned. Cut the dried apricots into smallish pieces and add to the pan. Add the pomegranate molasses, Worcester sauce and honey and stir until smooth. Now add the chicken stock and let the mixture bubble until it is reduced by almost half and thickened. Season to taste with salt and freshly ground black pepper.

Place the duck breasts, skin-side down, in a fairly hot frying pan. There is no need to add any fat – there should be plenty released as the duck breasts cook. Fry for 2–3 minutes, until the skins are golden brown, then turn over and repeat on the other side. Remove the duck breasts to a roasting dish and brush with honey. Season with salt and freshly ground black pepper. Roast for 12 minutes. Allow to rest and keep warm.

To serve, cut each duck breast into slices and fan them out in the centre of each of 4 warmed dinner plates (they are especially nice served on a bed of mashed celeriac). Surround with the Sticky Pomegranate and Wild Apricot Drizzle and scatter over a few fresh pomegranate seeds. Serve immediately.

preserved lemon and black olive drizzle
with quails in red peppers

Boneless quails nestling inside red peppers and served with this tangy drizzle, make a special and unusual dinner party starter or light lunch.

SERVES 4

for the drizzle

good handful of fresh basil leaves

2 tbsp fresh chives, chopped

1 clove garlic, crushed

1 tsp wholegrain mustard

pinch caster (superfine) sugar

½ large lemon

200 ml/7 fl oz/scant 1 cup extra virgin olive oil

peel ½ preserved lemon (see Larder Basics page 10), finely chopped

10 black olives, finely chopped

for the quails

4 large red (bell) peppers

salt and freshly ground black pepper

4 fresh tomatoes, quartered

1 clove garlic, crushed

8 home-dried tomatoes (see Larder Basics page 11), chopped

130 g/4½ oz goat's cheese, crumbled

2 tbsp pine nuts, lightly toasted

handful fresh basil, roughly torn

4 boneless quails

4 tbsp olive oil

Preheat the oven to 180°C/350°F/Gas 4.

To make the drizzle, place the basil, chives, garlic, mustard, sugar, lemon juice and olive oil in a processor and whiz to create a consistency similar to salad dressing. Add the preserved lemon peel and olives and stir. Season and set aside.

For the quails, cut a lid from each of the red peppers. Season the inside of each pepper with a little salt and freshly ground pepper. Mix the tomatoes with the garlic, season, then place 4 quarters in each of the peppers. In a bowl, combine the home-dried tomatoes, goat's cheese, pine nuts and basil.

Open up the quails and place a quarter of the cheese mixture into each, then roll the birds up. Carefully place a quail into each red pepper, season the tops and drizzle over a little olive oil. Place the peppers in a roasting tin and cook for about 30 minutes, until the quails are golden brown and cooked through.

To serve, surround each quail with Preserved Lemon and Black Olive Drizzle.

spicy tomato drizzle
with pan-fried salmon

In this spicy drizzle garlic and red onion huddle together in sticky
little puddles. Serve with a plump salmon fillet and a sprinkling of
freshly torn basil leaves for a mouthwatering meal. I have a favourite
shop-bought roasted-pepper olive oil that I use for this recipe – but
ordinary olive oil still works well – the result is just a little less spicy.

SERVES 4

for the drizzle

4 tbsp olive oil
1 small red onion, finely chopped
3 cloves garlic, crushed
4 tbsp good-quality tomato ketchup
5 tbsp pepper olive oil
handful of freshly chopped basil leaves

for the salmon

2 tbsp olive oil
4 x 175g/6oz salmon fillets, skin on
2 tbsp fresh lemon juice
salt and freshly ground black pepper

handful fresh basil to garnish

Preheat the oven to 190°C/375F°/Gas 5.

To make the drizzle, heat the olive oil in a pan, add the red onion and garlic
and sauté over a gentle heat until softened but not brown. Add the tomato
ketchup and cook for about a minute, stirring continuously. Gently pour in the
pepper olive oil and stir again. Season with salt and freshly ground pepper to
taste. Just before serving, add the freshly chopped basil.

Meanwhile, cook the salmon. Heat the olive oil in a heavy-based frying pan.
Add the salmon pieces, skin-side down, and sauté over a high heat for 2–3
minutes or so to brown and caramelize the skin. Turn the fish over, and cook for
a further minute. Transfer to an ovenproof tray, sprinkle over lemon juice, season
with a little salt and freshly ground pepper and cook for 6–8 minutes until the
salmon is cooked through but opaque.

To serve, place a piece of salmon in the centre of each of 4 dinner plates.
Spoon the Spicy Tomato Drizzle around, making sure to dot little mounds of the
onion and garlic here and there. Scatter with freshly torn basil leaves and
serve immediately.

creamy dijonnaise drizzle
with ham flakes on peas 'n' shoots salad

This recipe makes a lovely light lunch. Pea shoots are the tops from very young pea plants, but they can be difficult to find. So I grow my own! I bought myself a small, indoor propagator, sat it on a windowsill and threw in some pea seeds. Days later, I had my own supply of shoots. A green salad makes a nice alternative.

SERVES 4

for the drizzle

150 ml/5 fl oz/²/₃ cup crème fraîche

2 tbsp Dijon mustard

1 tbsp wholegrain mustard

zest and juice ½ lemon

2 tbsp clear honey

4 tbsp milk

2 tsp fresh tarragon, finely chopped

salt and freshly ground black pepper

for the ham flakes

250 g/9 oz/2½ cups plain flour, sieved

pinch salt

freshly ground black pepper

450 g/1 lb ham

1 egg, lightly beaten

for the salad

4 generous handfuls pea shoots

2 tbsp fresh young peas, shelled

handful sugar-snap peas

2 tbsp olive oil

squeeze fresh lemon

pinch caster (superfine) sugar

oil for deep frying

To make the drizzle, place the crème fraîche in a large bowl and add the mustards and lemon zest and juice. Stir to combine. Add the honey and milk and beat well. Add the tarragon and season to taste.

For the ham flakes, put the flour into a large bowl and season with salt and black pepper. Tear the ham into rough flakes. Dip the flakes into the beaten egg and toss lightly in the seasoned flour. Heat the oil to 190°C/375°F/Gas 5 and deep-fry, a few at a time, for 2–4 minutes, until golden brown and crisp. Drain on kitchen paper and keep warm until you have cooked all the ham flakes.

Place all the pea shoots, fresh peas and sugar-snap peas into a bowl, dress with a little olive oil, some lemon juice and a pinch of sugar. Season to taste.

To serve, place a mound of Peas 'n' Shoots Salad in the centre of 4 dinner plates. Top each with the Ham Flakes and serve with Creamy Dijonnaise Drizzle.

bloody mary drizzle
with roast sea bass

This drizzle is based on a sauce that I devised for the BBC *Master Chef* semi-final back in 1996. It has a lovely tomato flavour tasty with verve from vodka and a subtle kick of Worcester sauce. I hope you like it – the judges certainly did, because I won that day! Try to get sea bass fillets cut from a large fish, as the flavour will be far superior.

SERVES 4

for the drizzle

8 vine-ripened tomatoes
2 tbsp olive oil
1 tbsp good-quality tomato ketchup
2 tbsp vodka
1 tbsp Worcester sauce
90 g/3½ oz/7 tbsp butter

for the fish

2 tbsp olive oil
4 × 175 g/6 oz sea bass fillets (pinboned,
   with skin on)
juice ½ lemon
salt and freshly ground black pepper

fresh basil leaves and a handful of chopped
   black olives to garnish

Preheat the oven to 200°C/400°F/Gas 6.

To make the drizzle, place the tomatoes in a food processor and whiz until they are liquidized. Pour the mixture into a pan, passing it through a sieve to remove the seeds. Heat gently, then add the olive oil and tomato ketchup. Stir well, then add the vodka and Worcester sauce.

To cook the fish, heat the olive oil in a frying pan. Place the sea bass fillets in the pan, skin-side down, and cook for 1–2 minutes, until the skin is nicely caramelized. Turn the fish over and cook for a further minute. Lift the fish pieces out of the pan and transfer them to a shallow dish or roasting tray. Drizzle some lemon juice over each fillet and season with a little salt. Transfer to an ovenproof dish and place in the oven for a further 3–4 minutes, until cooked through – the flesh should be just opaque.

Gently reheat the drizzle and whisk in the butter, a little at a time, until fully incorporated. Check the seasoning and adjust if necessary.

To serve, place a piece of sea bass in the centre of each of 4 dinner plates, surround with the Bloody Mary Drizzle and garnish with fresh basil and chopped black olives.

red pepper drizzle
with little herb flans

Red pepper drizzle looks stunning on the plate and will complement
fish or poultry beautifully. Here I have chosen to drizzle it around
golden-yellow flans, flecked with fresh herbs, flavoured with tasty
Gruyère cheese and oven baked until set.

SERVES 4

for the drizzle

2 large, plump, red (bell) peppers, topped,
 tailed and deseeded
200 ml/7 fl oz/scant 1 cup well-flavoured
 vegetable stock
1 clove garlic, crushed
pinch sugar
1 tbsp balsamic vinegar
1 tbsp Worcester sauce
2 tbsp olive oil
salt and freshly ground black pepper

for the flans

4 whole eggs
4 egg yolks
175 ml/6 fl oz/³⁄₄ cup milk
175 ml/6 fl oz/³⁄₄ cup double (heavy) cream
1 small courgette (zucchini), skin on, coarsely
 grated
75 g/3 oz/³⁄₄ cup Gruyère cheese, grated
salt and freshly ground black pepper
2¹⁄₂ tbsp fresh mixed herbs (I use chives,
 parsley, chervil and a little French tarragon),
 finely chopped

You will need 4 × 200 ml/7 fl oz/scant 1 cup
ramekins lightly brushed with melted butter

Preheat the oven to 170°C/325°F/Gas 3.

To make the drizzle, place the red peppers in a food processor with the stock,
garlic, sugar, balsamic vinegar and Worcester sauce. Whiz until everything is
liquidized. Add the olive oil. Season well with salt and freshly ground black pepper.

Meanwhile, for the flans, whisk the eggs, egg yolks, milk and cream together in a
large bowl. Add the grated courgette (zucchini) and stir in the Gruyère. Add the
herbs and give everything a good mix round. Fill the prepared ramekins with the egg
mixture (giving it a stir to distribute the herbs and cheese as you go). Place them in a
shallow baking dish filled with water to come three-quarters up the sides of the
ramekins, and bake for 30–40 minutes or until set.

To serve, turn the Little Herb Flans out on to the centre of each of 4 dinner
plates and surround with Red Pepper Drizzle.

dark balsamic drizzle
with roasted pepper and feta salad

This drizzle consists purely of good-quality balsamic vinegar, and nothing else. Take some roasted red peppers, some crumbly feta cheese and black olives and you have a fabulous salad. Add a drizzle of balsamic vinegar, and you have a dish fit for the gods.

SERVES 4

for the drizzle

2–3 tbsp good-quality balsamic vinegar

for the salad

6 red (bell) peppers, topped and tailed
5 tbsp olive oil (I often use a chilli-infused oil for this)
2 cloves garlic, crushed
salt and freshly ground black pepper
250 g/9 oz feta cheese
12 black olives, pitted
handful fresh basil leaves

Preheat the oven to 200°C/400°F/Gas 6.

Cut the peppers into thin strips and place them in a shallow ovenproof dish. Drizzle over the olive oil, scatter with garlic and toss the peppers around until everything is nicely coated. Season with salt and black pepper. Roast for 30–40 minutes until soft and charred slightly here and there. Leave to cool.

To serve, arrange the pepper strips on a large, colourful serving plate. Crumble over the feta cheese. Scatter with the olives and basil. Drizzle over balsamic vinegar and serve at room temperature.

buttery caper drizzle

This drizzle is one of my favourites. Perky, flavourful and deliciously buttery, it complements smoky trout and bruschetta beautifully.

SERVES 4

for the drizzle

2 tbsp olive oil

3 shallots, finely chopped

1 clove garlic, crushed

300 ml/10 fl oz/1½ cups good-quality chicken stock

1 tbsp fresh lemon juice

3 tbsp double (heavy) cream

75 g/3 oz/6 tbsp cold butter, diced

3 tbsp fresh parsley, finely chopped

1 tbsp fresh chives, finely chopped

2 tbsp capers, roughly chopped

½ red (bell) pepper, finely diced

for the bruschetta

4 medium-thick slices bread cut from a good country loaf

3 tbsp olive oil

1 clove garlic, peeled

for the fish

375 g/13 oz young spinach leaves

1 tbsp butter

squeeze lemon

freshly ground black pepper

4 × 75 g/3 oz smoked trout fillets

Preheat the oven to 200°C/400°C/Gas 6.

To make the drizzle, heat the olive oil in a pan, add the shallots and garlic and sauté gently until softened but not brown. Add the stock and reduce by almost half. Stir in the lemon juice, followed by the double cream. Add the butter, a little at a time, stirring well until it is fully incorporated. Just before serving, add the parsley, chives, capers and diced red pepper.

For the bruschetta, brush the bread lightly with olive oil and bake for 10 minutes until golden and crisp. Remove from the oven and rub the garlic clove over each piece.

For the fish, wash and dry the spinach leaves and pop them into a pan with the butter. Cook over a medium heat until just wilted. Drain the spinach well and season with a little lemon and a grinding of black pepper. Keep warm.

Wrap the trout fillets in a piece of foil and warm them briefly in the oven.

To serve, place a bruschetta on each of 4 dinner plates. Top with spinach and lay the warm trout fillets on top. Surround with Buttery Caper Drizzle.

garlic cream drizzle
with sticky lamb chops

Smooth, velvety and full of delicious flavours, this is the ultimate drizzle to accompany succulent lamb chops that have been grilled to perfection with a sweet, sticky redcurrant glaze.

SERVES 4

for the drizzle

475 ml/16 fl oz/2 cups double (heavy) cream
6 whole cloves garlic
4–5 sprigs fresh thyme
2 anchovies
1 tbsp wholegrain mustard
salt and freshly ground black pepper
2 tbsp fresh parsley, finely chopped

for the chops

2 tbsp redcurrant jelly
2 tbsp Worcester sauce
8–12 medium lamb chops (depending on appetite!)

fresh parsley to garnish

To make the drizzle, pour the cream into a pan with the garlic and thyme. Bring to the boil, then turn down the heat. Simmer until the garlic is soft and the cream has reduced and thickened. Add the anchovies and stir until they have melted. Now add the mustard, and season with salt and freshly ground black pepper. Just before serving, stir in the parsley.

For the chops, mix the redcurrant jelly with the Worcester sauce and brush this over the chops. Grill for 5 minutes or so on each side, occasionally brushing with more glaze, until the meat goes shiny and sticky and is cooked to your liking. Remove from the heat and season to taste.

To serve, place 2 or 3 chops in the centre of each of 4 dinner plates and surround with the Garlic Cream Drizzle. Garnish with fresh parsley and serve immediately.

soured cream drizzle
with beetroot, raisin and red onion salad

This drizzle, made from the traditional accompaniment to *borscht*, the famous Russian beetroot soup, is soothing and subtle. I prefer my beetroot raw, grated and enlivened with lashings of fresh lemon, garlic and a scattering of sweet, plump raisins, but soured cream and dill still make an equally delicious accompaniment. I sometimes serve this drizzle over little stacks of *blini*-style pancakes layered with smoked salmon, for an elegant yet simple dinner party starter.

SERVES 4

for the drizzle

150 ml/5 fl oz/²/₃ cup soured cream
2 tbsp milk
2 tbsp fresh dill, finely chopped
salt and freshly ground black pepper

for the salad

4–5 medium-sized firm, raw beetroot, peeled and coarsely grated
2 cloves garlic, crushed
1 small red onion, finely chopped
50 g/2 oz/¹/₂ cup raisins
juice 1 lemon
pinch caster (superfine) sugar
3–4 tbsp olive oil

fresh dill to garnish

To make the drizzle, combine the soured cream, milk and freshly chopped dill in a bowl. Season to taste with a little salt and freshly ground black pepper.

For the salad, place the grated beetroot in a bowl with the garlic, onion and raisins. Add the lemon juice, sugar and olive oil and season to taste with salt and freshly ground black pepper. Turn into an attractive serving dish and, if possible, leave the salad to stand for 30 minutes or so before serving to allow the flavours to develop.

When you are ready to eat, trickle the Soured Cream Drizzle along the centre of the salad, garnish with fresh dill and serve immediately.

grand marnier drizzle
with little lemon creams

Grand Marnier Drizzle gives a beautiful deep orange gloss of flavour to anything it touches. I like it trickled over dark chocolate sorbet or fresh ricotta ice cream, but served with Little Lemon Creams it creates an exquisite dessert that never fails to delight. The liquid glucose in the drizzle helps to give it a smooth, shiny finish; buy it from large supermarkets, specialist cake-decorating or sugar-craft shops, or chemists.

SERVES 6

for the drizzle

1 tbsp liquid glucose

2 tsp caster (superfine) sugar

zest and juice 1 large, unwaxed
   orange

2 tbsp Grand Marnier liquer

1 tbsp concentrated orange juice

for the caramel

175 g/6 oz/¹⁄₂ cup caster
   (superfine) sugar

4 tbsp water

for the creams

200 ml/7 fl oz/scant 1 cup
   double (heavy) cream

6 tbsp milk

1 vanilla pod

3 eggs

3 egg yolks

115 g/4 oz/¹⁄₂ cup caster
   (superfine) sugar

zest and juice 2 lemons

for the moulds

2 tbsp melted butter

1 tbsp (approximately) caster
   (superfine) sugar

2 oranges, peeled and cut into
   segments, and fresh mint
   leaves to garnish

You will need 6 × 100 ml/3¹⁄₂
fl oz/scant 1 cup heatproof
moulds and a sieve lined with
butter muslin to strain
the custard

continued overleaf

Preheat the oven to 170°C/325°F/Gas 3.

Brush the moulds with the melted butter and sprinkle them with a fine layer of caster (superfine) sugar.

To make the drizzle, put the liquid glucose and sugar in a pan over a gentle heat and stir until the sugar has dissolved. Stir in the orange zest. Add the Grand Marnier liqueur and set it alight. When the flames subside, add the orange juice. Simmer gently over a low heat for a few minutes until the drizzle reduces and thickens slightly. Leave to cool.

For the caramel, put the sugar and water into a heavy-based pan and heat slowly until the sugar has dissolved. Increase the heat and boil rapidly, brushing the sides of the pan down with cold water on a pastry brush to remove any sugar crystals which could burn. Once the syrup reaches a dark caramel colour, remove from the heat immediately and carefully pour a thin layer of caramel into each of the prepared moulds.

For the lemon creams, place the cream, milk and vanilla pod together in a pan and heat until just beginning to bubble. Remove from the heat and leave to infuse. Meanwhile, whisk the eggs, egg yolks, sugar, and lemon zest and juice together in a bowl until everything is incorporated. Pour on the infused cream, whisking constantly until smooth. Strain through the muslin-lined sieve into a jug for pouring (this will make filling the moulds much easier).

Divide the lemon cream between the moulds and cover each with a small piece of foil. Stand the moulds in a roasting tin containing enough water to come three-quarters of the way up the sides of the moulds and cook for 40 minutes or until set. Remove the moulds from the roasting tin and leave to cool. Chill in the fridge until required.

To serve, turn a little Lemon Cream on to the centres of 6 serving plates. Garnish with fresh orange segments and mint and trickle over the Grand Marnier Drizzle.

passion fruit drizzle
with stag's breath ice cream

Tangy Passion Fruit Drizzle trickled over dreamy, creamy ice cream makes a fabulous combination. Stag's Breath liqueur is a glorious concoction of honeycomb and whisky, but if you have difficulty getting hold of it simply substitute your favourite creamy whisky liqueur.

SERVES 4

for the drizzle

6 passion fruits
1 tbsp concentrated orange juice
1 tbsp caster (superfine) sugar
2 tbsp water

for the ice cream

4 1/2 tbsp caster (superfine) sugar
150 ml/5 fl oz/2/3 cup water
4 egg yolks
300 ml/10 fl oz/1 1/2 cups double (heavy) cream
5 tbsp Stag's Breath liqueur

fresh mint and orange zest to garnish

You will need an ice cream machine

To make the drizzle, cut the passion fruits in half and scoop out the seeds and pulp into a food processor. Whiz for 10 seconds or so to help release the juice from the seeds. Sieve the mixture into a small pan, reserving some of the seeds. Add the orange juice, sugar and water and heat gently until the sugar has dissolved. Stir in a few reserved seeds and set aside to cool.

For the ice cream, put the sugar and water into a pan and heat gently until the sugar has dissolved. Bring to the boil and bubble for 2 minutes. Whisk the egg yolks in a large bowl and slowly pour the hot syrup over the egg yolks, whisking all the time. Continue whisking until the mixture is pale, has doubled in volume and has cooled (this will take up to 10 minutes). In another bowl, lightly whisk the cream and Stag's Breath liqueur together. Fold the cooled egg yolk mixture into the cream and freeze in an ice cream machine.

Serve the Stag's Breath Ice Cream in pretty bowls, with Passion Fruit Drizzle, and garnish with a little mint and fresh orange zest.

raspberry drizzle
with clotted cream and raspberry tart

This is a beautiful drizzle and perfect to make in late summer, when raspberries are plentiful, plump and flavoursome. It is lovely over ice creams and sorbets, but do try this gorgeous tart of creamy golden custard with juicy sweet raspberries, all encased in crisp hazelnut pastry.

SERVES 4

for the drizzle

250 g/9 oz/1½ cups fresh ripe raspberries
2 tbsp Framboise liqueur
4 tbsp caster (superfine) sugar

for the pastry

250 g/9 oz/2½ cups plain (all-purpose) flour,
  sieved
pinch salt
90 g/3½ oz/½ cup hazelnuts, toasted and
  chopped
175 g/6 oz/¾ cup butter, softened

65 g/2½ oz/⅓ cup caster (superfine) sugar
1 large egg yolk

for the filling

250 g/9 oz/1 cup clotted cream
3 large eggs, beaten
150 g/5 oz/¾ cup caster (superfine) sugar
1 tsp vanilla extract
200 g/7 oz/1 cup fresh ripe raspberries

handful extra raspberries and mint leaves to
  garnish, and icing sugar to dust

You will need a 25 cm/10 in loose-bottomed
tart tin

Preheat the oven to 190°C/375°F/Gas 5.

To make the drizzle, whiz the raspberries in a blender or food processor to purée, then sieve to remove the seeds. Add the Framboise liqueur and sweeten the purée with caster sugar.

Now make the pastry for the tart. Place the flour, a pinch of salt and the chopped, toasted hazelnuts in a bowl. Set aside. Beat the butter and sugar together with a wooden spoon until creamy. Add the egg yolk and stir until smooth. Slowly fold in the flour and hazelnuts and turn through gently with your hands until the pastry forms a ball. Wrap it in cling film and leave to rest in the fridge for 20 minutes or so.

For the filling, whisk together the clotted cream, beaten eggs, sugar and vanilla extract. Set aside.

continued overleaf

Roll the pastry out to line the tart tin (you may have some left over, but this will freeze beautifully for another day!). Take special care to make sure that there are no holes in the base – the hazelnuts can sometimes disguise little gaps! Chill for 30 minutes. Bake blind (prick the pastry case all over with a fork and cook without the filling) for 10–15 minutes until pale golden and crisp. Reduce the oven temperature to 170°C/325°F/Gas 3. Set the tart tin on a baking sheet (this makes it easier to carry to the oven after pouring the filling into the pastry case). Sprinkle the raspberries evenly over the tart base, then carefully pour in the custard mixture. Place in the oven and bake for 30–40 minutes until set. Remove from the oven and leave to cool.

Serve the tart in slices, and surround with a little drizzle. Garnish with a few extra raspberries and a sprig of fresh mint, and dust with a little icing sugar.

lemon grass drizzle
with chocolate sushi

Lemon Grass Drizzle has a subtle but sophisticated flavour. It provides the ideal delicate accompaniment to dark Belgian chocolate wrapped around sticky rice, flecked with piquant lemon zest and studded with exotic fruit.

SERVES 4

for the drizzle

2 stalks lemon grass
150 ml/5 fl oz/²⁄₃ cup water
90 g/3½ oz/7 tbsp caster (superfine) sugar

for the sushi

75 g/3 oz pudding rice
550 ml/18 fl oz/2½ cups milk
50 g/2 oz/¼ cup caster (superfine) sugar
zest 2 lemons
75 g/3 oz dried papaya
50 ml/2 fl oz/¼ cup double (heavy) cream
115 g/4 oz dark Belgian chocolate (55% or
    more cocoa solids ideally)
pared zest 1 orange (remove with a potato
    peeler), very finely sliced
2 tsp fresh mint, finely chopped

To make the drizzle, remove the tougher outer layer from the lemon grass and discard. Using a large kitchen knife, bash each stalk of lemon grass along its length and then chop very finely. Pour the water into a pan and add the caster sugar and lemon grass. Bring to the boil and then simmer gently for 3–4 minutes until the syrup has thickened slightly. Remove from the heat and set aside to allow the syrup to cool and the lemon grass to infuse.

For the sushi, place the rice, milk and sugar in a large bowl and microwave on high for 20 minutes, stirring from time to time (or cook the rice in a pan on the hob for 20 minutes if you prefer, or if you do not have a microwave oven). Stir the lemon zest into the cooked rice and leave until completely cold.

Stir the papaya into the cold rice. Whisk the cream until stiff and fold this into the rice mixture.

Melt the chocolate in a bowl over a pan of gently simmering water. Cover 2 flat baking sheets with cling film, making sure that the film is pulled tightly across the surface so that there are no wrinkles. Spread the melted chocolate in an even layer to form 2 rectangles of about 23 × 14 cm/9 × 5½ in. Pop them in the fridge until the chocolate has just set but is still slightly pliable.

Now take the rice mixture and form it into 2 23 cm/9 in long rolls. Place 1 roll across the centre of each chocolate rectangle then very carefully pull up the chocolate around the rice and pinch together at the top, so the long ends of each rectangle stick together. You should now have 2 long tubes. Return to the fridge until set hard.

When the chocolate has set, remove from the fridge and cut each tube into 6 even pieces. I like to cut the tops on the diagonal to make the presentation especially effective. To do this, start with a diagonal cut then a straight cut, and alternate until you reach the end.

To serve, place 3 Chocolate Sushi in the centre of each of 4 pretty dessert plates. Top with the finely sliced orange peel. Surround with the Lemon Grass Drizzle and sprinkle with freshly chopped mint leaves.

cactus-pear drizzle
with lime ricotta ice cream

I am always reminded of Walt Disney's *The Jungle Book* whenever I use cactus pears. They are, after all, the renowned prickly pears that Baloo and Mowgli sing about. Cactus pears have a soft, mellow flavour with soft flesh and edible crunchy seeds. The colour of this drizzle is dazzling, and when served with the pale but zesty Lime Ricotta Ice cream it makes an eye-catching dessert.

SERVES 4

for the drizzle

2 cactus pears
juice 1 lemon
2 tbsp caster (superfine) sugar
1 tbsp grenadine

for the ice cream

300 ml/10 fl oz/1½ cups milk
4 egg yolks
175 g/6 oz/7/8 cup caster (superfine) sugar
juice 3 limes
250 g/9 oz/scant 1¼ cups ricotta cheese
7 tbsp double (heavy) cream

fresh mint and lime zest to garnish

You will need an ice cream machine

To make the drizzle, peel the cactus pears and put the flesh into a food processor with the lemon juice, sugar and grenadine. Whiz until smooth. Sieve to remove the seeds, transfer to a bowl and store in the fridge until required.

For the ice cream, heat the milk gently in a pan until just below boiling point. Meanwhile, mix the egg yolks with the sugar. Pour the hot milk on to the eggs, stirring all the time with a wooden spoon. Return everything to the pan and cook over a low heat, stirring constantly until the mixture is thickened sufficiently to coat the back of the spoon. Stir the lime juice into the ricotta and double cream and then whisk this thoroughly into the warm egg mixture until smooth. Leave to cool, then freeze in an ice cream machine.

Serve the Cactus-Pear Drizzle over the Lime Ricotta Ice Cream and garnish with fresh mint and a little lime zest.

red wine and anise drizzle
with buttered pear puff

Simple and yet striking, this is a glorious drizzle, combining fruity
red wine with a gentle nip of anise, sweetened and simmered to a
glistening syrup. It is very special served with crisp, buttery pear puffs
but is also superb served over lemony ice cream.

SERVES 4

for the drizzle

1 bottle fruity red wine (claret works well)
250 g/9 oz/1¼ cups caster (superfine) sugar
2 whole pieces star anise

for the puffs

275 g/10 oz puff pastry
2 plump, firm, ripe pears (such as Comice)
1 tbsp fresh lemon juice
40 g/1½ oz/3 tbsp butter, melted
3 tbsp demerara sugar

vanilla ice cream or crème fraîche to serve

Preheat the oven to 200°C/400°F/Gas 6.

To make the drizzle, place the wine, sugar and star anise in a pan. Bring to the
boil, stirring to dissolve the sugar, and then lower the heat. Let the mixture bubble
until the wine has reduced and has the texture of a light syrup. Set aside to cool.
Take care not to let the wine reduce down too much because it will thicken more
as it cools.

Meanwhile, roll the pastry out to a thickness of about ½ cm/¼ in and cut into
4 squares. Prick the central area of the pastry gently with a fork. Peel the pears
and remove the cores. Cut each pear in half and then cut each half lengthways at
intervals, about ½ cm/¼ in apart, leaving the stalk ends intact. Fan the pears out
slightly, brush them with a little lemon juice and gently place a half-pear on each
of the 4 pastry squares. Trim the pastry around the pears, leaving a 1 cm/½ in
border. Now score gently around the edge of each pear, using the point of a knife,
without going right through the pastry. This will help to create a raised border as
the pastry cooks. Brush the pears and pastry with melted butter. Sprinkle a little
sugar over each pear and cook for 15–20 minutes, until the pastry is golden
brown and crisp and the pears are nicely glazed.

To serve, place a Buttered Pear Puff in the centre of each of 4 special dessert
plates and surround with Red Wine and Anise Drizzle.

tipsy butter drizzle
with hot banana splits

Tipsy Butter Drizzle is sweet, luxurious and laced with dark rum, rather like slightly boozy molten toffee.

SERVES 4

for the drizzle

75 g/3 oz/scant ½ cup soft brown sugar
3 tbsp good-quality cider vinegar
4 tbsp dark rum
90 g/3½ oz/7 tbsp butter

for the icecream

6 egg yolks
175 g/6 oz/⅞ cup caster (superfine) sugar

2 plump vanilla pods
450 ml/15 fl oz/scant 2 cups milk
300 ml/10 fl oz/1¼ cups double (heavy) cream

for the bananas

1 tbsp vegetable oil
4 ripe, firm bananas

4 tbsp pecan nuts, toasted and coarsely
   chopped, to garnish

You will need an ice cream machine

To make the drizzle, place the sugar and cider vinegar in a pan over a gentle heat. Stir until the sugar has dissolved. Add the rum and set it alight. When the flames subside, add the butter, a little at a time. Remove from the heat and set aside.

For the ice cream, place the egg yolks in a bowl and add the sugar. Cut the vanilla pods open down the centre, but leave the top ends intact. Scrape out the seeds and add to the egg- and-sugar mixture. Stir well until the mixture is smooth and light. Put the milk and vanilla pods into a pan and heat until just below boiling. Pour the hot milk into the egg mixture and stir. Carefully pour everything back into the pan and stir constantly over a gentle heat, with a wooden spoon until the custard is thick enough to coat the back of the spoon. Remove from the heat. Add the double cream. Leave to cool, then freeze in an ice cream machine.

For the banana, heat the oil in a griddle pan until hot but not smoking. Cut the bananas in half along their length and place on the griddle. Cook for 2–3 minutes until golden and charred. Turn over carefully and repeat on the other side.

To serve, place 2 halves of banana in the centre of each of 4 dessert plates. Put 2 scoops of ice cream in the hole the banana-halves create. Surround with Tipsy Butter Drizzle and sprinkle with chopped pecans.

apricot drizzle
with chocolate soured cream cake

Light and fruity, this drizzle takes only seconds to make and contains just two ingredients. In fact, you could say it's a real doddle of a drizzle! This is another great one for ice creams and sorbets, but is fabulous served with this elegant, dark chocolate cake.

MAKES 1 CAKE/SERVES 4-6

for the drizzle

350 g/12 oz jar good-quality apricot conserve
175 ml/6 fl oz/³/₄ cup dry, fruity white wine

for the cake

200 g/7 oz good-quality plain chocolate
120ml/4 fl oz/¹/₂ cup crème fraîche

130 g/4¹/₂ oz/²/₃ cup caster (superfine) sugar
5 eggs, separated
50 g/2 oz/¹/₂ cup finely ground almonds
1 tbsp cocoa powder

icing sugar to dust
crème fraîche to serve

You will need a 20 cm/8 in cake tin, the base lined with greaseproof paper and oiled

Preheat the oven to 180°C/350°F/Gas 4.

To make the drizzle, place the apricot conserve and the wine in a food processor and whiz until the mixture is smooth. Set aside.

For the cake, put the chocolate in a bowl and place over a pan of gently simmering water until the chocolate melts. Allow to cool and then stir in the crème fraîche, half of the caster sugar, egg yolks, almonds and cocoa powder. Whisk the egg whites and remaining sugar until stiff. Stir a couple of tablespoonfuls into the chocolate mixture to loosen the mix, then gently fold in the remainder. Keeping the mixture light. Turn the mixture into the prepared cake tin and bake for 40–50 minutes until a skewer inserted into the centre comes out clean. Remove from the oven and leave in the tin to cool completely.

To serve, turn the cake out, dust with icing sugar and serve cut into slices with Apricot Drizzle and a dollop of crème fraîche.

blackberry drizzle
with crushed meringue creams

Luscious, inky blackberries are among my favourite soft fruits. Add a glug of Crème de Mûre (blackberry cream liqueur) and a touch of sugar for great results. Crisp, sweet meringues and chilled crème fraîche complete the picture, in a dessert that is loosely based on Eton Mess.

SERVES 4

for the drizzle

500 g/1¼ lb/3 cups plump fresh blackberries
50 ml/2 fl oz/½ cup Crème de Mûre liqueur
  (or Crème de Cassis)
50 g/2 oz/¼ cups caster (superfine) sugar (or
  to taste)
1 tbsp fresh lemon juice

for the meringues

3 egg whites
pinch salt
175 g/6 oz/⅞ cup caster (superfine) sugar
200 ml/7 fl oz/scant 1 cup crème fraîche

fresh mint to garnish

Preheat the oven to 110°C/225°F/Gas ¼.

To make the drizzle, place 300 g/11 oz/1¾ cups blackberries into a food processor together with the Crème de Mûre liqueur, sugar and lemon juice. Whiz and taste – you may have to add more sugar, depending on how sweet your fruit is. Press the mixture through a sieve, to remove the pips, and set aside.

For the meringues, whisk the egg whites, salt and sugar together until stiff peaks form when you lift the whisk out of the mixture. Place tablespoonfuls of the mixture on a baking tray lined with baking parchment, and bake for 1½ hours. Reduce the heat if the meringues are browning rather than drying out. Remove from the oven and leave to cool. Store in an airtight tin until ready to serve.

To serve, take 2 meringues and crush lightly with a fork. Loosely fold in a quarter of the remaining blackberries and a quarter of the crème fraîche. Pile into the centre of a cheerful dessert bowl. Pour the Blackberry Drizzle around the meringue and a little over the top. Garnish with fresh mint. Repeat with the remaining fruit and meringues in the other dessert bowls.

index

Acknowledgements

With grateful thanks to Colin and Vivien at Pavilion, who took my dream and brought it so beautifully to life. To Maxine, my editor and the rest of the Pavilion team working busily in the wings, with thanks for all the hard work – and for being such a great bunch to boot!

And if it is that diamonds really are a girl's best friend, then here are some of my most precious.....

Geraldene Holt for her constant support and encouragement along the way. My fellow 'Sparkies' at the Guild of Food Writers, for so freely offering advice when asked! A whole host of good friends that have tasted, tested and always come back for more! My wonderful parents and two brilliant brothers and their families – who were always ready and willing to sample with a smile and so generous with their love and support. And my four very special 'tasters' at home – David, Chris, Oliver and Tim.